Nectar of Nondual Truth

CONTENTS

10 Essence of Advaita Vedanta, Part 3
by Dr. Alexander Hixon
The final installment of Lex Hixon's three talks on Advaita Vedanta finds him selecting and commenting on a few of the choicest and most engaging slokas of Gaudapada's famous Karika on Nonduality, replete with examples of realized souls who exemplify it and words about those who pretend or misunderstand it.

17 Jain Monasticism
by Swami Brahmeshananda
Continuing onward with his thorough and most informative series of articles on the peaceful religion of the Jains, all based upon his own direct past experience of them while on pilgrimage to their holy sites in India, Swami Brahmeshananda delivers deep insights into both the life and history of the monks of this exemplary world religion.

22 Memorizing Scripture
by Annapurna Sarada
The yogic tradition of Svadhyaya, recitation and memorization of slokas and sutras of the revealed scriptures of India, is given an indepth and hands-on inspection in this article, revealing it as an indispensable spiritual tool and discipline for the sincere aspirant after Truth.

27 Householders, Sadhana, & Spirituality
by Babaji Bob Kindler
The collapsing family life of present day society, and the unfortunate fragmentation of mind that causes it, can be rendered whole once again by the implementation of time-tested spiritual disciplines into daily life.

32 Menschcraft
by Rabbi Rami Shapiro
Careful observance of the challenges of everyday life play an important part in many of the religions of the world, such as maintaining a strict moral stance in Christianity, adherence to the dharma by chaste Hindus, and the mindfulness practices of various Buddhist schools. Judaism is no different in this regard, being well-known for encountering and dealing with life in the world in a joyful and balanced fashion.

38 A Return to Christian Advaita
by Father Bruno Barnhart
This reprint of Father Barnhart's offering on Christian Advaita, as seen in Nectar of Nondual Truth, Winter, 2002, is placed here in honor of his passing on November 28th, 2015. His connection to India's non-dualism is instanced in his words, *"Unitive Reality lives at the heart of the Western spiritual traditions, but it has rarely been expressed there with the directness and purity with which we find it in the Hindu and Buddhist literature."*

40 Physics and Vedanta
by John Dobson
Before he passed away in January of 2014, our beloved Vedantic spiritual brother said: *"Space is not that which separates the many, but that which seems to separate the one. And in that space that Oneness shines, therefore falls whatever falls."*

42 Ethics and Spirituality
by Swami Aseshananda
Notably, there is a marked difference between ethical life and dharmic life. Whereas the former sets up the latter so that the precious dharma can work on the important level of religious life, the enforcement of ethics alone, devoid of knowing what lies beyond them, can be a substantial block to spiritual progress.

49 Zen Principles & Distractions
by Babaji Bob Kindler
The razor's edged spiritual path can be more easily and successfully navigated if advance notice of certain impositions known to past masters are heeded early on. In this brief article, which utilizes an explanatory chart of several of these obstacles, common but aggravating impediments to Zen practice are noted, reminding the aspirant to stay the course and remain on vigil.

"As Vedanta reminds us over and over again, throughout these many cycles of manifestation in the realms of becoming, only knowledge of the intrinsically pure and unalterable state of our innately complete nature can provide us with perfect health, perfect mental well-being, perfect religious harmony, and a perfect nondual philosophical stance attended by a fully conscious perspective."

Publisher's Page

Sarada Ramakrishna Vivekananda – SRV Associations
"Setting the feet of humanity on the path of Universal Truth."

Notes on an Advaitic Journal

At the basis of Advaita as the philosophy of Shankara and his gurus, there is Advaita as experience. Advaita as experience represents that supreme place where all diversity merges in its Essence. It is not combatant or immiscible with qualified or dualistic approaches, but rather provides them their place of consummate arrival. Where actual practice rather than mere book learning is emphasized, where religion, philosophy and spirituality are not separate from one another, where knowledge and love, reason and devotion, are never divorced from each other, there does the truth of authentic nonduality effloresce.

Historically speaking, experiential Advaita originated with the ancient Rishis. Therefore, the Upanisads contain the nondual truths of the Vedas which declare: idam mahabhutam anantam aparam vijnanaghana eva, *"This great Being is endless and without limit. It is a mass of indivisible Consciousness only."*

SRV Associations & Universality

The SRV Associations are part of a worldwide movement of spiritual aspirants devoted to the study and practice of Vedanta and Divine Mother Wisdom. The ideals of this ancient pathway to God, exemplified in the lives of Sri Sarada Devi, Sri Ramakrishna and Swami Vivekananda, are the original and eternal perfection of the Soul and its inherent oneness with Reality, the manifesting of divinity in our lives, selfless service of all beings as God, and reverence for the ultimate unity of all sacred traditions. To this end our purpose is to study, worship, and contemplate Truth so that spirituality may flourish. This is the Advaitic way — *"None else but Self, none other than Mother."*

Nectar's Mission — Advaita-Satya-Amritam

In Sanskrit, *amrita*, nectar also means Immortality – and this is, indeed, what we are offering: opportunities to become aware of this Amrita that is our very Essence via the rarefied teachings from Vedanta and the World Religions and Philosophies that appear in each issue of Nectar.

Nectar of Non-Dual Truth is SRV Associations' heartfelt offering of highest Wisdom to the human community. It is the sincerest form of love and service we know to disseminate non-dual Truth and teachings which transmit pure knowledge, pure love, and true universality. Through Nectar we are working out SRV's mission of spiritual upliftment and education. Please join us; this is a universal movement.

Keeping Nectar in Print

Nectar is a free magazine that can be ordered in printed form online at www.srv.org, and it can also be viewed online. (play.google.com/books) However, substantial donations are needed every year to maintain this publication in print. Why is this important?

1 – Printed Nectars are best for person to person and organization to organization dissemination of these ennobling teachings that deepen one's own spiritual life and engender knowledge of, acceptance, and reverence for all other paths.

2 – Only printed copies can reach those who do not have access to online viewing, including prison inmates, who are a particular focus of SRV's social seva.

Use the subscription/donation form provided at the back of this issue to send a check or credit card payment to SRV Associations, P.O. Box 1364, Honokaa, HI., 96727, or donate online at www.srv.org. Your donations are tax deductible.

With reverent gratitude, we heartily thank the contributing writers of this issue of Nectar of Nondual Truth, who have so graciously and selflessly shared the wisdom of their respective traditions and practices.

Staff of Nectar of Nondual Truth

Publisher
Sarada Ramakrishna Vivekananda Associations
an Annual Publication
For more information concerning the SRV Associations or Nectar of Nondual Truth please contact:
SRV Associations, PO Box 1364, Honoka'a, HI 96727
Phone: (808) 990-3354
e-mail: srvinfo@srv.org   website: www.srv.org
Nectar Subscription is on a donation basis only

No part of this publication may be reproduced or transmitted in any form without permission from the publisher. Entire contents copyright 2016. All Rights Reserved. ISSN 1531-1414

Editor
Babaji Bob Kindler

Associate Editor
Annapurna Sarada

Production
Lokelani Kindler

Cover Image:
Prakasha Ben Cavalcanti

Harmony of Religions Image used by permission of the Vedanta Society of St. Louis

Acknowledgement
Image of Ramakrishna's Disciples Courtesy of Vedanta Press
800-816-2242

Contributing Writers
Swami Aseshananda
Swami Brahmeshananda
Dr. Alexander Hixon
Father Bruno Barnhart
John Dobson
Rabbi Rami Shapiro
Annapurna Sarada

EDITORIAL

It remains somewhat of a mystery, even after all the advantages of contemporary times have been lavishly bestowed upon present day humanity, that the ills of pervasive suffering still persist on the world scene. Of course, we know from the Buddha's declaration of His Four Noble Truths, that suffering here on Earth will never go away entirely. Still, unnecessary suffering, a type of misery that has viable solutions, also remains constant — despite the fact that humanity has had plenty of time to apply these readily available stopgaps. When looking at this perplexing situation, the conscious observer cannot but notice, often painfully so, that narrowness of mind lies at the root of both the problem of suffering itself, and its tardy removal.

In view of all this, when one considers ultimate solutions, there is nothing that compares with that of Universality. Universal religious outlook, universal philosophical perspective, universal compassion, universal service of mankind, a more universal mindset — even a more universally-based business and politics — all would be welcome alternatives to the ponderous and ineffective arsenal of methodical weapons that nations and peoples are presently utilizing to try to stem the tide of pervasive human suffering. True, religion nowadays has become an obvious caricature of itself, and philosophy has turned into a job and a career instead of a means for the revelation of truth. Even altruistic service, after the many attempts it has made towards drying up the ocean of human misery, has shown us its limitations and its downside.

But all of these only need to turn to the original state from which they emerged so long ago. In other words, the ultimate solution of solutions lies right in front of and within us. As Vedanta reminds us over and over again, throughout these many cycles of manifestation in the realms of becoming, only the intrinsically pure and unalterable state of our innately complete nature can provide us with perfect health, perfect mental well-being, perfect religious harmony, and a perfect nondual philosophical stance attended by a fully conscious perspective. Peace of mind lies there, what to speak of the "Peace that passeth all understanding," and both will lead to the closest proximation of peace on earth that is possible in any given age and time. For an indepth look at Universality, its superlative forces, and qualification for its uses for highest good, my article called *The Open Arms of Religious Congeniality*, featured in the January, 2014 issue of *Prabhuddha Bharata*, can be consulted.

For those who, as yet, still cannot comprehend or envision such a harmonious and universal world, the means towards doing so lies in opening the mind up after ridding it of barriers such as selfish grasping, hatred, and delusion. The cultivation of generosity, kindness to others, and gaining insight into the nature of both relativity and Reality, will accomplish this feat. A downpouring of sterling virtues and an infilling of powerful currents of darkness-destroying light into the freshly opened avenues of the mind will be the welcome result. No real healing work can be accomplished on the collective level without this removal of root obstacles that stand in the way at the individual level.

Importantly, living beings of all nations and sincere adherents of every religious tradition must become the recipients of these newly opened channels of universal mind and their well-intended modes of selfless service. The heretofore unhealthy modes of darksome thinking that were plagued by jealousy, the desire to dominate, and the urge to commit violence, must dissolve in the light of a clearer understanding that perceives the one, indivisible Consciousness abiding in all living beings — what the Vedanta calls *Atman*, or *Paramatman*. As the *Chandogya Upanisad* puts it: "Prana springs from Atman, aspiration from Atman, memory from Atman, Akasha from Atman, fire from Atman, water from Atman, appearance and disappearance from Atman, food from Atman, strength from Atman, understanding from Atman, contemplation from Atman, intelligence from Atman, will from Atman, mind from Atman, speech from Atman, name from Atman, hymns from Atman, rites from Atman — all this and more springs from Atman alone."

Om Peace, Peace, Peace.

Babaji Bob Kindler

NECTAR OF ADVAITIC INSTRUCTION

Questions from Our Readers

"The light bestowed upon the seeking mind by Atma-vichara outshines all other lights, and disperses darkness like a thunderbolt on a stormy evening. Even the murky depths of mula-avidya, root ignorance, is dispelled by the coruscating light of Atma-vichara."   Lord Vasishtha

"I was tuned in for this past Sunday's live-streaming class, and at some point you asked a question related to one of the Great Master's sayings. It is the following: 'If my devotees know who I am, who they are, and what the world is, they will be fine.' Then you asked the audience who we are, and one lady replied 'Brahman,' and you corrected her saying, 'Atman.' My question is related to this, since it is mentioned in some texts that Atman equals Brahman, or that this Self is Brahman. Can you please elucidate on this?"

This question surfaces every once in a while in conjunction with the idea that Vedanta has more than one word for Reality, i.e., Atman and Brahman. You might already have heard that Brahman is the formless expanse of pure, conscious Awareness, Divine Reality per se. Atman is that same expanse temporarily or apparently limited by form. It is like filling a jar with water from an ocean, then placing that jar in the ocean. There is water inside and water outside. The water inside is Atman, the jar is the ego mind-mechanism that limits it, and the ocean is Brahman. One will have to break the jar under water for the limited One to become the Limitless One – but it is all water, nonetheless.

Every dewdrop glistening on the grass in the early morning has a glint of the sun within it, but the entire sun remains transcendent of all those millions of drops. It is reflected light from the standpoint of the individual drops, but it is all one indivisible Sun from the sun's perspective. To rise to such a perspective (samadhi) is rare and wondrous.

So, for an individual "dewdrop" (like the woman who answered "Brahman" in class) to declare that it is the entire sun is a bit ambitious on its part, yes? Sri Ramakrishna used to say that it is not good for the householders, and those who are still busy with the world and its affairs, to declare, "I am Brahman." It will take a very special and powerful dewdrop, or a fully transparent jar, to take up a position of such an advanced nature.

We, as individuals, need to work on realizing "I am the Atman within, not the body/mind mechanism." As we expand our understanding, and then our capacity for enlightenment, we will then be able to say with all assurance, "I am the Atman in all." Thus, there are stages to realization, and we want to move through them with full comprehension in order to return to that ultimate Being that we never parted from in the first place. We only dreamed ourselves to be a separate being. Until we awaken from that dream we are to cling to the Atman (not the world) with all the force and power of our burgeoning realization.

Once, just as I am writing to you now, Swami Vivekananda wrote to one of his woman disciples who was prematurely taking up the "All is God" stance in a letter (All is not God; God is All). He composed in his return letter a spontaneous poem for her, the last verses which read:

So, Mary Hale, allow me tell —
You mar my doctrines, wronging, balking,
I never taught such queer thought
That all was God — unmeaning talking.

But this I say, remember pray,
That God is true, all else is nothing!
This world's a dream, though true it seem.
And only Truth is He the living!
The real me is none but He
And never, never, matter changing!

"In relation to eating habits, what to eat and what not to eat, I have stopped eating red meat for about a year now and then stopped eating chicken and turkey for some few months. What is your advice on this matter in relationship to being on a spiritual path? I ask this because I have found myself to be able to cut these foods, meaning that I don't desire them much, but I have noticed recently that I have been feeling weak physically, with stomach problems. I'm not sure if it is related to my not eating meat and chicken. So what are your thoughts on the kind of food one should or should not eat in order to progress spiritually? Is it true that when one eats animals, that person is incurring bad karma? How important is the topic of food when it comes to observing the yamas of Yoga when one is a spiritual aspirant?"

It is very commendable that you have given up eating denser meat. That you feel you do not need it, and do not desire it, is a sign that you are doing the right thing. That you feel weak, and the stomach feels unsettled at times, is also a sign. But it does not necessarily mean that meat gave you strength before; it is more that your system got used to eating it before, and is now trying to adapt to a finer fare. I have not eaten meat for over forty-five years and I never feel lack of strength. But I can remember having trouble digesting meat in my teens, and that took away strength from my life and actions.

So go ahead and experiment further with this new precedent. I would advise fish if you feel your system requires a bit denser food. Women, especially, can benefit from fish.

About karma and eating animals, yes, karma will be there. One has to deal with it, like with all karmas. This is a karma-bound world. But we cannot expect the people living near the North Pole to give up eating meat; they have no other food there. For them, it would not be "bad" karma, then, but just karma. The seal has its karma for being born a seal, the Eskimo has his karma for killing and eating the seal, and there would be a karma to pay if the Eskimo did not kill the seal in order to feed his family and thereby let them starve. All around us is karma, on all sides. We must learn to reduce it to a minimum so that it will give us less resistance along our pathway; that is all. We should not lose our sensitivity for life either, and that happens if we eat animals indiscriminately – like the people of the world are doing today.

So, in conclusion, we should try to reduce our karma, and also make a statement to others about being careful, concerned, and cautious with regard to all other beings on the planet.

"In the first sloka of the Vivekachudamani, Sankara says that Brahman can only be known through knowledge of the scriptures. In making this statement is he simply saying you need knowledge that leads to realization? This statement isn't to be taken to the point of meaning jnana yoga is the only path or only thing needed to get to God, right?"

Yes and no. Without jnanam and scriptures it will not be possible to realize the Formless. But God with form can be approached by other paths, i.e., works, devotion, faith, sacrifice. God's Grace may also do it, but who has had that Grace without some knowledge of Reality to begin with or, put another way, if ignorance has not been destroyed? God, the Reality, is not present where ignorance exists. That is why, as Vivekananda has stated: *"God is not in the world; the world is in God."*

How can we know God if we are deluded? We may be able to have devotion to God if still deluded, and pray for God to take it away, but for Him to do so will require our participation in the process. It is like if you would ask God, "Lord, will you take away this delusion for me?" And He would answer, "Okay, but first you must do this one thing I ask." As Sri Ramakrishna has said, you cannot lay hands on the book at the bottom of the stack without taking off all the books on top. Seeing God is quite like this. You must remove some obstacles, impediments, overlays, coverings, superimpositions, etc. That is the work of Jnana Yoga. In brief, without some kind of spiritual discrimination, how is it possible to see God — who is Ever-one, Formless, and Perfect?"

"On another note, I was reading *Astavakra Samhita* and the text I found had no commentary. I was first surprised to see that it is a relatively short scripture. But what struck me is the teachings there, which are purely non-dual. What I'm trying to say is that the sage Astavakra imparts to King Janaka the non-dual Truth and Janaka, just by hearing the Truth, is liberated without any need for him to go through spiritual practices. In the text, the sage emphasizes in different places that the dull-witted person desires to attain liberation by reading the scriptures and meditation and goes into a struggle, while the wise one, upon being told the non-dual Truth, neither desires to attain liberation nor struggles, but rests in the glory and peace of the Self. So the teachings in the Astavakra Samhita are certainly directed to certain types of souls, and not everybody. Is this correct? I'm assuming King Janaka was a highly evolved soul to be able to realize the Truth at once. Can you comment on this?"

King Janaka and Astavakra represent one of those divine couples that are rare, but when contemplated, explain the subtleties of spiritual life and realization. Later, King Janaka turns around and informs Sukadev of the highest Truth, and he gets illumined all of a sudden as well. This sudden enlightenment actually comes about for a soul who has already done all the purifications and austerities that have prepared him/her for it. Nondual scriptures of this kind, as rare as they are, thus have no commentary. They impart the highest wisdom directly, and if the soul is qualified to hear it in just the right way and at the auspicious time, then illumination occurs. This was the way in the olden days too, when the guru whispered the mantra into the ear of the disciple and samadhi occurred. Today there is far too much conditioning and overlay in the minds of beings for this to happen. A lot of training and de-programing has to happen first. Today the path is to clarify, then intensify — and there are very few people who want to take even this method up.

"How is Pratyahara practiced?"

The fifth limb of Yoga is most important, and is where most practitioners of the day fall down in their practice of Yoga. Defined as detachment, more specifically it is drawing the five senses back from their desired objects using the burgeoning will of the mind. This has two forms: first, one has to do it on the physical plane by checking one's life and habits and seeing to what extent one is attached and unable to exist without certain objects and amenities. When one finds a thing or pleasure that is overbearing or, in this day and age especially, distracting, then it must be withdrawn from for awhile until one can take or leave it at any and all times.

Secondly, once external detachment is achieved, one begins to examine the source of attachment, which lies in the mind. Pratyahara here is drawing back from thoughts that distract one from concentration (the sixth limb of Yoga) on teachings, Ishtam, and/or Brahman. When the mind settles easily and swiftly on what Patanjali calls the "desired sacred object," then is internal pratyahara mastered.

Notably, the objects of the world have come from the mind's ability to project unmanifested nature (Prakriti) into form. Objects are thought made concretized. If this is true, the mind must also remember that it can also dissolve what it solidified. Ironically, it does so every night in the dream state. Now, all distractions and attachments can depart the mind, leaving it in a calm and blissful state — which was its original condition before embodiment.

One may question more on this limb of Yoga, but it should also be practiced in life (the external) and in meditation (the internal).

"In *Yoga Vasishtha,* the sage Vasishtha says: 'The sage of infinite vision sees in the one undivided Intelligence countless universes, for he has realized the magic of Maya or cosmic illusion. He sees the infinity in every atom, and therefore he is unattached to the rise and fall of the ideas of creation. Hence, he is ever contented with what comes unsought (which he doesn't reject) and he does not run after what has been taken away from him, for which he does not grieve.' Will you please comment more on this, and in particular, explain what is meant by the sentence, 'He sees the infinity in every atom, and therefore he is unattached to the rise and fall of the ideas of creation.' What atom is he referring to? The physicist's atom?

The mental condition of the seer is incomparable and enviable, once it is perceived. The "nectar of naturalness" abides in him/her. Peace is a given there. Bliss is coming and going in him all the while, independently. Part of the reason for this is his singular look into the nature of outer phenomena. He has seen its particles, or that it is all consisting of particles. The scientist has seen this in the case of the physical atom, but has not inspected his own thoughts to find that they are made of particles of intelligence. Food has particles of prana in it, but few know of it, and think only of the pleasure it brings, the energy it bestows, and the health it supplies. Thus, awareness brought to the subtler areas of creation will open up avenues heretofore unknown to most of mankind on Earth.

But the real advantage the luminary has is in his knowledge of the changing and the Unchanging. He will not accept change to be real, for, as Jesus said, one should not build their house on "sand." It has to be built on "bedrock." "Rock of Ages" is not a type of music; it is Divine Reality realized as the underlying substratum of all of Existence.

So, if you were to see without a doubt that atoms, molecules and other physical particles are based in constant change, and you were really intelligent, what would this tell you? What conclusion would you make? You would first confirm the illusory nature of objects, then you would go forth and find the basis upon which this change is taking place. A dancer needs a stage. So, what is the stage for all of this dancing of particles that is going on? And if I can find none such in the physical, then I must ask what is the nature of the cosmic dance? And finally, where is rest, where is stasis, where is peace, or where does this frenetic dance end and the Dancer Himself, see Himself? This is Self-realization. Its process can be conducted in the midst of change, but its conclusion has to be confirmed in the static atmosphere of Changeless Reality Itself. As my guru used to say, "You cannot realize the Infinite through the finite."

"My other question is about the difference between heart and mind in the following sentence, once again from *Yoga Vasishtha:* 'With a pure heart and a receptive mind, and without the veil of doubt and the restlessness of the mind, listen to the exposition of the nature and the means of liberation, O Rama.' I remember you mentioning in your live-streaming classes that people talk about the heart all the time, and that in this context, they are really talking about their mind. And that the 'real' heart is not the anatomical one, but it is the fourth chakra and the abode of the Lord. So coming back to the above sentence from Yoga Vasishtha, what is meant by the heart when he says '....with a pure heart?' And is it different from the mind? And what does it mean to say that the fourth center/chakra is the abode of the Lord, 'the drawing room of the Lord,' as the Master used to mention repeatedly?"

Pure Heart and Pure Mind are, to the Vedantist, the same principle. According to Sri Ramakrishna, they are also God. Overlays and superimpositions, conditionings and modifications, limitations and imperfections, veils and obscurations — all of these are as if nothing to the Pure Mind, what the Buddhists refer to as the "Original Mind."

And this is precisely why the heart chakra (*anahata*) and the third eye chakra (*ajna*) have an indivisible connection with one another. Ordinary aspirants tend to think that the chakras are lower to higher. But they are outer to inner, and once the "inner" is reached, there is no real degree of dimension to be seen. It is sort of like losing direction in outer space — where is South, where is North?

This cosmic body of God is not so divided and disconnected as the human form. In the latter, or Virat, the eye is in the forehead, true, but its gaze is always lowered to the centers of eating, drinking, and sex life. In Vishva, God's internal body, all functions are everywhere and all connections are immediate. There is no disjointed features or random and sporadic actions. The weight of matter has been lifted off, and buoyancy of Light is everywhere. Thus, one will find the third eye in the heart, and the heart in the third eye! It is like molding a clear wax figure while fashioning a red heart right into its head.

Back on Earth, then, this heart chakra provides a meeting ground for God and the devotees, and the third eye chakra allows for them all to approach and experience higher visions while still in the body — drawing room and a high gable! Where else shall we go? Where else can the devotees "hang out?"

"I read in the elucidation that every soul is Divine and that every living being has a Divine birthright. A question here comes to me; what is meant by a living being? Does it mean humans, animals, plants as opposed to table, rock, etc.? I'm confused also when it is said that all objects are thoughts made concrete, projections of the mind; what is meant here by objects? Are they things that are not alive in the common sense of the word alive? For example, is a dog a mental projection? This might sound like a stupid question, but for me it is a valid one. Does a dog have a soul? What about a tree? A rock? I hope you get the gist of this question."

Everything is really divine in origin, since it all comes from Cosmic Mind, or AUM. But in the case of the human being, this inner divinity can be awakened and realized, then expressed. That is what we see and hear in the cases of the seers and luminaries. We do not see any other "living" beings expressing such Light, such Bliss, such Wisdom: only them.

So, all living beings such as plants, insects, and animals, live by prana, or life force; few of them live by intelligence. Even among human beings there are precious few who have developed higher Awareness. Dogs may have souls of a sort, and other animals too, but there are no realized animals. It is in the human form where that blessing takes place, and nowhere else. If animals are taken under wing by people, say, like Ramana Maharshi's cow, then a better lifetime may be in store for them in the future. Even that is somewhat rare, for all that most cows do is eat grass all day. Even most humans often fail to get realized, so how then an animal?"

The Atman exists in all beings equally in quality and quantity. What is not equal amongst the species is the degree of Its manifestation. Sunlight shines best on a mirror, and fine on a lake, but not so well on a leaf or a rock...."

"Surely, fear will be transcended at the time of realization, but before that it has to be managed. So, for the aspirant, not the apta, would you address the management of fear?"

If one can train the mind to think of nothing but Divine Reality all the time, then where are things like anger, fear, lust, and the other problems people complain about? Tulsidas, the divine poet of South India, puts it this way: *"O Ram, this is my prayer to Thee: kindly destroy my mind's tendency to perceive duality. For Atman alone abides; none else exists. It is attachment to relativity that gives birth to the miseries of life."* Notice how he blends awareness of nonduality with intense devotion to Ishvara. Is there a better path for the jiva?

But others may not be able to comprehend such subtleties of spiritual life. From the perspective of the soul/aspirant who lets fear rise, I could venture to say that short of just being with the Self as Brahman, there is a second option of making sadhana the ground upon which one can manage fear. That is, if one is still in the trenches, battling dualities and adverse tendencies coming from karmas and samskaras, etc., then learning to handle fear, subjecting it to terms of attenuation dictated by the mind controlled by spiritual self-effort, will be the next best thing.

For instance, one can wash it away with the heart's devotion to Ishvara; one can fight it off by recitation of the mantra; one can meditate it away by staring it straight in the face from the Witness standpoint of the Atman within; one can even work it away, using this otherwise useless body and its fluctuating energy in the service of the deathless Lord and Mother Who abides in all beings, all things.

Then, of course, there is the path of discrimination. Seeing death and the fear that arises from it in the light of what is real and unreal is a surefire method to send it back to the primal ignorance from which it springs. And if one repeats this time and time again, whenever fear comes up, it will be quiet after a time and not bother one anymore. And in fact, when one uses this method of sadhana, all the ways and means mentioned above have got to be actuated under the press of a constant regimen. Perseverance is king in this court.

One of Swami Aseshanandaji's talks appears in an earlier issue of Nectar, #29. Take another look at it. It is titled, "Facing our Fear."

"Is interpreting dreams where spiritual beings appear important? I had a dream recently where I was sitting and taking teachings in a gymnasium from Swami Aseshananda. As the class ended he said that we needed to close because the space used for the class was reserved for Babaji and his sangha."

The fact that spiritual beings even appear in your dreams is a fine thing. For most dreams occurring at this level, that is better than interpretation, or as good. It shows how deep the teachings and teachers have gone inside of you — in your case, in a very short period of time. I also had a "gymnasium" dream early on. All three of our Ideals were laying on a raised stage, apparently deceased. Then all of a sudden Sri Ramakrishna sat straight up, and in my dream I stood up from my seat in the audience and cried out, "Jai Sri Ramakrishna!"

"My sister is in a fierce struggle for survival right now, and it keeps on getting worse every time it seems to be getting better. My question is, how can I keep my calm in the face of this suffering — a calm, I might add, that is suitable for effective yogic practice. Holy Mother said the first thing we need is peace. I question what value a peace that rises and falls with situations has; there must be at least some steadiness to it. You've said to people who are excessively concerned, 'Well, just stop being so concerned!' I find that this reduction of concern is needed! I could be of better help to my sister if I could be less concerned. I'm exploring ways to be less concerned, starting with seeing everything my sister goes through as an expression of her karma. I'm not doing this in a hard-hearted way. This is helpful but it's not enough. What other attitudes — what mental asanas — can I adopt to keep my calm and peace?"

The advaitic answer to your question, "How can I keep my calm?," is, "One should never lose one's calm in the first place," or, "It is not an option to lose one's peace of mind." Concern, yes, of course; that will be there unless one truly is hard-hearted. Grief at loss, too, is natural in the short term, unless one is unattached to everything. Still, though a full-fledged sannyasin of the highest order, Swamiji felt loss keenly with regard to his monk brothers, disciples, and his Guru, etc.

But these realized souls are another matter, and their methods of dealing are so refined and advanced. We can look at them as examples of where to be, but more pertinent to our own state of advancement, or lack thereof, we must take the dharma teachings and apply them to these situations that arise in our lives. More advanced beings control themselves so that there will not be any additional aggravation heaped upon our already pitiful condition during trying times — more gloom piled on gloom, as Swamiji wrote in a poem. Besides, later, after all the pathos and weeping is over, light always comes, and the Mother shows Herself in some ready form to lift up our hearts and give us bliss. We then understand that the former object of our sorrow — a person, situation, condition — turns out to be fine in another realm.

But back to the teaching of keeping our calm, that needs practice. Where are we going to get such practice if not under fire, if not in this life, in this embodied condition, in these difficult circumstances? To be born is to face death, no doubt. But how will we fare when our time comes?

One key I can give you, which is also a measure. If, after examining your sorrow, grief, fear, etc., you find that it is really based upon fear of your own death, of your own suffering, then you know where you have to work — within your own mind. But if you find that your concern is wholly for the other, that you feel for them in their time of trial and not only for yourself, then there is the measure and the key — the key being that by thinking of others all the time, and never for yourself, you naturally avoid the brooding around all impending challenges that people worry about, even from their young age.

This is the definitive "practice" that *"makes fear afraid of itself, and puts death in its own grave,"* as Ramaprasad sings.

"Can you please elaborate on the statement below from 'How to know God' by Swami Prabhavananda and Christopher Isherwood? It was written that 'Non-attachment is the exercise of discrimination.'

This is a good connection to make for the aspiring jnani. Knowing about this viveka and putting it into practice makes up the first step, and detachment comes next. Though detachment has some ten or more levels — from meek to middling to intense — the end result will be mature non-attachment (*paravairagya*). This is also called mature renunciation. Sri Ramakrishna is the best example of this quality in recent memory.

First, it must be said that non-attachment is not indifference. Neither the aspirant nor the onlooker should judge renunciation/detachment/non-attachment prematurely or unjustly. Only very shallow minds will defer to pointing the finger at detachment and calling it callousness, etc.; dharma teachers are always careful to point a finger in a different direction so as to indicate how mature and full of compassion and understanding detachment truly is.

Further, it is only when one is in possession of such detachment that true compassion, love, and selfless service can be expressed and rendered. Otherwise, and it is always the case, living beings often make a muck of everything, including relationships, work, and life in general, due to their inadvertent attachment to all and sundry. The common misconception that one has to be "involved" to really be loving, to be empathetic, and to be effective, is an idea for the weak-minded. Being "aloof" from this mess that humanity has gotten itself into is a sign of spiritual advancement, not otherwise, and provides a definite advantage to the spiritual being. This position is really the only way to help bound living beings figure out how to get themselves out of such debilitating emotional troubles."

"Can you fill in some of the gaps on my understanding of 'contemplation' versus 'thinking'? I see thinking as the mind being the 'boss,' and being directed by ego and running the show unconsciously, whereas contemplation is being more focused and directed at God; it originates from a deeper place than mind. And what about 'desire' (for God, for example) versus 'want?' In both these cases, how does one distinguish whether it is one or the other that is occurring — assuming one is more desirable than the other?"

In Vedanta, the mind is fourfold — *manas, chitta, buddhi,* and *ahamkara,* or, mind, thoughts, intellect, and ego. When we say "mind," here, it means the doubting mind; not just ordinary doubts that everyone has, but the major doubt concerning the existence of Reality or not. Since manas, also called dual mind, is always focused on the world, and on pros and cons, pleasure and pain, and other "deluding pairs of opposites," it forgets God, and the result is suffering and ignorance.

The fourfold mind is called *antahkarana* in Sanskrit, the "inner cause" of all things. Vedanta, and Indian Philosophy overall, does not believe in a God that creates (i.e., you cannot create something out of nothing), but rather that the mind projects the universes in space and time. There is a cosmic mind, or Mind of God, if you will, and there is also a collective mind which is the composite mind of all beings such as humans, ancestors, celestials, gods and goddesses, etc.

With this much outlined and clarified, we can take up the difference between contemplation and thinking. To the seers of India, these two are much the same act, only contemplation is on higher thoughts while thinking is often set on ordinary or lower thoughts — even mundane thoughts and evil thoughts (*klistha vrittis*). This is all intermediate psychology. The real difference to be looked at, then, is the difference between contemplation and meditation. In the latter, thought (ideally) tends to slow down and even disappear (*samadhi*). Thus, a well balanced spiritual life is based in keeping the mind on higher thoughts (*aklistha vrittis*) while moving through daily life, and simultaneously going into meditation when sitting to do daily practice.

Basically, desire and want equal the same thing. But you mention the desire for God-realization; that is not a desire in the ordinary sense of the term. What needs to be distinguished, as Holy Mother has taught us, is the difference between desires that quicken dispassion for the world, and desires that stimulate enjoyment. The former kind are sought after in spiritual life and striving, and the desire to realize God falls highest among these.

The refinement of viveka is the answer to the third part of your query. *Viveka* is the discrimination between the real and the unreal, the essential and the nonessential. By honing it one soon sees with crystal clarity all the many illusions of maya, as well as all the separate delusions of the mind in maya. Once spirituality begins to dawn in the individual, these differences will become obvious.

Write in if there are any more questions concerning this subject. This process, called *Atma-vichara,* is the main mental practice in higher spiritual life. The guru is present for this one exercise, mainly, and much gets accomplished in the interim as well.

"I have a question from this past Sunday's live-streaming class. You mentioned that it is easier for humans to realize the Atman than for the deities. Why is it so?"

The idea is that the gods, having obtained their high position in the internal worlds, are fixed there for an indefinite period of time. As you may have heard, the Atman is nameless and formless; realizing It places one's consciousness beyond the worlds of name and form. Thus, it stands to reason that if the human being can realize the Atman in this very lifetime, he/she can transcend the realm of the gods and unite with Formless Reality, i.e., Brahman.

"Recently I read that Sri Ramakrishna said that those who confused his bodily appearance with Him knew Him not at all, that He was the essence that lived inside. This got hold of me. It kept coming to mind over and over until finally I decided to try modifying my meditative technique on the basis of the Master's statement. As I chanted my mantra, I experimentally abandoned efforts to meditate on Thakur's form and instead

thought of Him as Atman. A powerful meditation subsequently followed. I've never been a good visualizer. Ideas are my province, not visualizations, and this suited me rather well. It also occurs to me that this shift in technique mixes a huge dose of jnana into my bhakti, and furthermore does it in an integrated way. The long and short of it is that I feel inclined to work with this more, and I'd like to know what you advise."

I have often noted the two different temperaments of aspirants, and explained them as visionaries and mystics. The former have inward visions and the later proceed by vibration, like AUM and the wisdom vibration. The advantage in the mystical types is that they are less impeded by form, and can therefore move more easily through barriers of form to get to the formless Essence. Of course, some visionaries are not susceptible to attachment to form, and only use it to "....get to the Father through the Son." Nevertheless, all this applies, case by case.

As for your experience, it is obviously time for you to step out and try such a journey — a journey out at sea after striking off the moorings that bind the ship to the docks. The port and docks are always waiting anyway after the mariner perceives the endless ocean and experiences such blissful, peaceful vastness. The comparison here is really between the bliss of form and the bliss of formlessness. It is rather like icebergs in the ocean: the former are Majestic, *Mahima*, while the latter is Infinite, *Ananta*.

"Would you address Swami Vivekananda's understanding of full enlightenment? What does it involve in terms of both inner realizations and outward behavior in the world? Would you clarify how it differs from older, more traditional understandings of enlightenment in Vedanta? And how does Swamiji's understanding of full enlightenment differ from Shankara's, if it does differ?"

His experience of full Enlightenment was a realization and not just an understanding, and it was so full-blown and flexible that it covered all the stages of the meaning of the word, i.e., like *krama mukti*, *jivanmukti*, and *videha-mukti*. But probably what you ask about here is called *Sarvamukti* — liberation at all times for all souls. This is not an attainment, but rather an eternal state of pure Awareness that is the true nature of Reality — a Reality that at some point seemingly breaks into parts and, in the process of returning back to their Source, begin to seek for immersion in that Essence. In Swamiji's estimation the soul is born free, lives free, and passes from the body free, and returns to its ever-present Freedom — and all the while the coming and the going is "pure nonsense." He could not see any other way to it, and would not accept any. This is an ever-free Soul, what Sri Ramakrishna called him when he first laid eyes on him in that lifetime — a *Nityasiddha*.

As far as Shankara and Vivekananda are concerned, I see so many correlations in the two of them that they might as well have been incarnations of each other. However, the times were different in 700 A.D. than when Swamiji came in the 1800's. In short, times are darker now spiritually speaking, notwithstanding and maybe even because of the dawn of the technological age, so a different approach was needed to uplift the masses.

And Swamiji took that approach. We are still uncovering and understanding it, even today. One facet of it, for instance, is that Swamiji saw that many of the people of his time were not going to be able to realize God due to so many karmas and weights. Therefore, He proposed a path by which, and I paraphrase, the *"most amount of beings could make the greatest amount of spiritual growth in the shortest amount of time."* He said that we may not be able to gain enlightenment individually, but that we can gain it in a general sense as a concentrated body of beings if we pull together.

This was a part of his thinking as he gazed out from his eternal moksha state upon the human race in the Kali Yuga in the 1800's. Will humanity get it together and pull together for a higher common end? If what he brought to the world in the form of the Vedanta is imbibed and implemented into life, then it is more probable.

"How does the aspirant sincerely offer their work to the Lord?"

It is not a matter of how, but rather that one must; otherwise, the taint of selfishness and the problems of a self-serving nature will increase, and can never be overcome. The dynamics, however, are subtle. All the four main yogas must be made into vehicles for sacrificial offerings. Take a look again at the early chapters of the Gita, how Sri Krishna explains them, and what order they come in from Him.

First, there is Arjuna's dejection (symbolizing that all souls must suffer in this world); then comes the yoga of basic knowledge or dharmic life. Next is how to act; this is followed by the ability to renounce action in the knowledge one has already gained. Then, complete and mature renunciation arrives. All this is followed by meditation or, in other words, one can finally meditate after putting all the former impediments to route. This comprises the first six chapters of the Gita, said to be the "karma" section. The next six are the "bhakti'" section. The final six are the "knowledge" section.

"Is there a single best practice of pranayama? The reason for this question is due to various readings and listenings about different ways of doing pranayam. The latest one was the Soham-Hamsa from *The Avadhut* book. But I also recall one discussed in a cd discourse when Shankara commented on the 8 limbs of Raja Yoga, and it also being discussed in relation to japa in the book, *Reclaiming Kundalini Yoga*."

The overall best mode of pranayama is the advanced one, which is also the one that few arrive at, they being satisfied with those forms that merely pump the heart and give excitement, etc. It is best to use pranayama to locate the prana, then master it; that is the whole point. The mind (i.e., knowledge) must be involved for this to occur, for beyond the physical prana lies the psychic prana, and that is more pertinent to Enlightenment rather than to pranayama's lesser gifts — especially those of health, longevity, and occult powers. To breathe consciously while focusing inwardly in knowledge is a much more beneficial practice than breathing out and "through the body" only.

Questions, observations and insights regarding problems in spiritual life or the issues of the day may be directed to Nectar's editorial staff at srvinfo@srv.org and will be duly addressed in succeeding issues.

◆ Dr. Alexander Hixon

ESSENCE OF ADVAITA VEDANTA

Exploring Gaudapada's Nondual Philosophy, Part 3

This is the third and final talk on Gaudapada's Karika that Lex Hixon presented in the late 1980's.

In non-dualistic experience we become transparent as it were — the walls of the world and of any sort of conceptual base or perspective we have. It all becomes clear without disappearing, yet still remaining functional. Everything becomes transparent because nothing is arbitrarily separated from anything else.

The Zen masters say that if you can't express your realization in words, then you haven't had realization. That sounds very strange because we think of Zen as very anti-intellectual, maybe even anti-verbal — but it is not so. My good friend and Zen teacher, Bernie Glassman Sensei, a Western sensei, was a Ph.D. in mathematics and that was one of the reasons he was so brilliant in solving koans. A mathematician has to see basic underlying patterns, and be able to pick them out, to be able to identify them clearly — so clearly that he could even make a formula of it. Then the pattern wouldn't appear random or be only occasionally recognizable, but in some way one could always recognize it. Bernie used this ability in solving koans. The illumined intellect or the intuitive intellect is something very important in spiritual life. In the case of mathematics, one must have the ability to describe an insight in mathematical language. In our case, we have to be able to describe realization in English, and in relatively ordinary English as well.

I thought we might look at Book Two as a whole and try to say simply what it is all about. Then those who are reading the manuscript and thinking about it can ask questions for clarification. There is always a danger of this becoming a philosophical thing that one merely thinks about. When you can think yourself into the philosophy, suddenly it makes sense, but the rest of the time it may remain somewhat vague. Mathematics could not work suitably that way, as if a mathematician had to be in some sort of high state of consciousness to understand his mathematics. It has to be something that is crystal clear all the time. And this is also a factor in spiritual life and the path of knowledge, called Jnana Yoga. Granted this takes years, but we can begin seeing that ideal; it shouldn't be vague, it should be crystal clear.

The Existence of Awareness

So the basic teaching of Gaudapada is that what exists is an infinitely subtle complex network of perspectives of awareness. The whole thing, as it were, Reality, I've translated here as the panorama of Consciousness. It is an open panorama. Sometimes it is even called the "Open Panorama," and sometimes in Book Two it is the "Clear Light of Consciousness." In Book Three Gaudapada develops the notion of calling it "Empty Space" or "Limitless Space." These are just words, but as I said earlier, words are important. They are the way we really describe this understanding. If we can't put the understanding into words, we don't have it. It's a very strict thing. We might have wonderful feelings and intuitions, and sometimes feel very high and other times feel very low, but Jnana Yoga should be crystal clear and expressible, obviously, without limiting it. We are not going to put it into some sort of conceptual framework. Gaudapada's whole premise is to loosen us and release us from our various types of conceptual frameworks so that this Open Panorama of Consciousness appears through the vast myriads of perspectives of the entire universe.

There is a fundamental dual structure of awareness called experiencer and what is experienced — roughly, subjects and objects. So awareness is always dual, but that is not some sort of debility. That is not some sort of terrible mistake that has to be eradicated. It is just the way awareness works. It is just the way perspectives work.

So what he suggests is that the persons he calls the sages, the great silent ones, are those who have awakened as the whole Panorama. But for them none of the perspectives necessarily disappear at all. If a sage were sitting in this room, he or she would be fully aware of the traffic outside, and would be fully aware of everyone here inside, and with much more of a sense of differentiation and distinctness and carefulness of perception than we have, because we are too caught up in our perspectives. We're identified with our perspectives, for example, with the perspective we call "me." Therefore, we really can't be so fully and richly and generously aware as the sage is. The sage doesn't have identification with any of the particular perspectives in that sense. It is just that he or she is awake as the entire Panorama and so would be aware of the suffering of the five billion human beings on earth, a few of them being here in this room. But the sage would be very much aware of the suffering of those beings plus all sorts of other living beings, sentient beings. The sage would be very much aware of all of their longings and aspirations and would be feeling great solidarity with all beings. So it is never a question of, "it is all an illusion." This is something we have tried to fight against from the very beginning — this false understanding of the non-dual wisdom of the sage, that "really all this is an illusion, a strange persistent illusion." Let's all rethink this. Are there any questions or comments before I go on? Is this clear, what is being presented?

Q: "In being so aware, the sage is not necessarily suffering, is he?"

That is very important. The sage is not "awareness." Awareness always has a dual structure. It is always perspectival. The sage has awakened out of awareness, has awakened as the entire Panorama of Consciousness. Also, he or she is aware, obviously. The sage could smell a flower and be aware that it is fragrant. So the sage does have awareness and perspective. If the sage was sitting in that chair, he or she would be very much aware that the flowers were to their left, not to their right. I mean, the sage doesn't make any mistakes of perspective and the sage does not kind of wander around in a daze. But as all of Consciousness Itself, as Gaudapada says, the sage is at perfect peace. So indeed, he or she is not suffering in the same way as beings who are caught within their own play of perspectives. The sage is definitely free from suffering in that sense. But how does he or she use this freedom? By being even more compassionate, and by being more aware in a warm way. One might say that the sage suffers for others, but the sage him or herself would not necessarily accept that.

We use Mother Teresa of Calcutta as the best example of the non-dual sage that we can think of. She is contemporary. She doesn't come from Hindu or Buddhist tradition, she comes from a Western Christian tradition. This shows that non-dualism is not something that is confined to an Eastern philosophy. It would be wrong to say that she is caught in the suffering of the world. She is free, but she feels the suffering. Yet it is not "for others" because for her there are no "others." As she would say, in her non-dualistic way, "There is only Christ." A very realized Krishna worshipper would say "There is only Krishna." But since Christ was crucified, a great sensitivity to suffering has developed in Christianity, whereas a devotee of Krishna might be more attuned to bliss, the bliss of Krishna.

God, His creation, and his devotee, are perspectives of awareness. What really exists is this vast Panorama of Consciousness, which I think is exactly what the great devotee of the Lord experiences actually, in the ultimate penetration or the ultimate exaltation. He or she doesn't really experience a kind of separate God and a separate soul and their play together. — although "the play of soul and Lord" is one perfectly valid way of describing the whole thing. Gaudapada is really attempting to get beyond religion without ever invalidating religion as a marvelous human activity. If we don't get to some more fundamental basic point than religion then we are at the mercy of these disagreements between the religions. This is, just autobiographically, one of the reasons I started this class. I felt I was at the mercy of the differences of the religions. I have connections with different religious traditions and I'm constantly feeling drawn this way and that way. Just for my own sanity, my own health of mind, I had to try and find some way, a basis, out of which one can be religious — Jewish or Christian or Hindu or whatever. However, as I have said before, I don't believe that one can just be a "Gaudapadist."

The Two Wings of a Bird

I was talking with a sister here who was saying she felt she needed bhakti as much as jnana. In other words, she felt she needed the full picture. I agreed entirely. Someone who just says, "I am a jnana yogi," or "I'm just interested in the ultimate philosophical meaning and not in devotion or rituals or anything like that," is missing the point. It is, I think, the non-dual understanding that gives a base, a strong basis for compassionate activity, for devotional activity, or for discipline of various kinds. Then there is a kind of unshakable basis that it is placed upon. This is getting back to the idea of having a crystal-clear basis.

Religions have their own kind of very clear basis. Any discipline, any body of knowledge, tries to present a very clear basis. Now, the problem is, we are in a world where there are different religions; there are different bases that are being presented and they conflict with each other. So what are we going to do under these circumstances? Are we just going to wonder about it, or not worry about it, or sometimes be Jewish and other times be Buddhist? How is humanity going to deal with this? I think that something like the wisdom of the non-dualistic sage has to come into play now. This may have more relevance now — for a global civilization — than it has ever had before. This is another reason why we are taking the time to examine this great text so closely and think about it. We think this might have a very profound relevance for the modern world.

The Uniqueness of a Nondual Scripture

It amazes me sometimes how sophisticated this text is. It is almost like we are studying super pure mathematics or advanced physics. We've seen how these very advanced disciplines such as physics can gradually begin to have an effect on people's thinking. In the world there are just a handful of people who are actually advanced physicists, who know all the mathematics and everything necessary to really see what is going on there. But it seems to be beginning to have an effect on the whole general thinking of others — intellectuals and artists. Gaudapada is really much more advanced than modern physics. Modern physics is still an empirical science; it doesn't pretend to be a total vision of reality. It doesn't represent the illumination of human consciousness and a total unfolding of its potentiality and possibilities. This text does represent that. There is so much interest in the new physics and all that. I wonder if there would be that much interest in this, which is basically so much more pertinent to the human condition. The new physics is not meant to be a world-view for the whole human race to live in, as it were. But that is why we are paying attention to this text. I'd like to write a book on this text and just see what the interest would be.

The European renaissance was kindled by a specific thinking around the rediscovery of certain Greek texts. This was part of the kindling of an entire movement in a culture. I think it would be very, very fruitful for the approach of non-dualism to be discovered by a culture. We'll see. We're not exactly filling up this room with vast numbers of people who are interested in it.

The Old Rope Trick

Let's be a little more specific and talk about Gaudapada's basic analogy that he gives now. He's very reluctant to give analogies, but he does offer one here — the famous old snake-and-the-rope. We can call it the old rope trick.

The dimly perceived rope at twilight that lies across the forest path is imagined in various benign or ominous forms as a small stream, or as a poisonous serpent. This is similar to the Clear Light of Consciousness, or the Open Panorama of Consciousness, dimly perceiving life through dualistic awareness. When we think that there is some sort of fundamental separation between the experiencer and what is experienced, it makes for a kind of dim, murky atmosphere. This is the sort of twilight that we are in — *"seeing through a glass darkly,"* as Saint Paul says.

> "The European renaissance was kindled by a specific thinking around the rediscovery of certain Greek texts. This was part of the kindling of an entire movement in a culture. I think it would be very, very fruitful for the approach of non-dualism to be discovered by a culture."

And he continues to say, *"Then we will see face to face."* But Gaudapada wants us to see face to face right now. He states:

The Clear Light of Consciousness dimly perceived through dualistic awareness is imagined in the form of various structures and its true nature is thus misunderstood. Advancing further along the path, the true nature of the rope is revealed with clarity......

Seeing clearly does not necessarily take any special effort on the part of the onlooker. If you just come closer, you become more intimate with the reality and it reveals itself most clearly. If it was deep twilight, the villager would be trembling. If he would get within a few feet of the presumed snake he would see very clearly that it was only a rope. And once one sees that it is a rope, such knowledge is irreversible. One doesn't go back and think, "Well, maybe it is a snake" again. There is a point where it is absolutely clear, and this is enlightenment. It can't be reversed. In Buddhism, some beings are referred to as "irreversible bodhisattvas." They have seen that they exist only for others, lifetime after lifetime. And there is nothing, nothing that could happen which would make them lose that understanding.

So, advancing further along the path, the true nature of the rope is revealed with clarity. The vivid perspective of the dangerous serpent fades. And it is vivid. Think about the times that we've been afraid — that vividness. The vivid perspective of all this traffic, as some sort of form or structure, fades.

And the villager joyously exclaims, "This is just a rope and nothing else!" Similarly, awake as Clear Light, the sage exclaims with delight, "The world is the Panorama of Consciousness and absolutely nothing else."

So, it is a delightful experience. It is a kind of relief. We gaze out at Broadway, or we gaze at the busy-ness of our own lives, and understand it as the Panorama of Consciousness and nothing else. Does that change anything? No. Do we quit our job and move to Acapulco? No. Do we stop suffering? Not necessarily. We might even suffer more as we become more sensitive. We are no longer confined by the dualistic perspective, so we are actually more open to everything. Gaudapada continues:

The Demise of False Projections

Habitually, we ignorantly structure the Open Panorama of Consciousness, thereby misinterpret its true nature as breath, life, energy, or countless other structures.....

A philosopher or physicist might look at the world and say, "It is energy." Gaudapada is saying it is not energy. That would be like saying that the rope is something like a little stream going across the path. It is just not its nature. It is not the true nature of the Panorama of Consciousness. Further, he states:

The universal process of structuring arises automatically from the perspectival functioning of awareness.....

This is very important to note: perspectival reality is like an automatic function of awareness. It is not something wrong; it is not something we should stop perceiving. Even the illumined sage doesn't stop perceiving a world with various things happening in it.

Ramana Maharshi is another great example of the nondual sage. One time he saw a dog that was chasing a squirrel and he turned and threw his staff in between them and distracted the dog while the squirrel went up a tree. But he fell down and broke his collarbone. This is a beautiful image of non-dualism. Here is a person who had no subject-object consciousness, who wasn't structuring the world in any way, but spontaneously acted out of compassion. He paid the price of the action by breaking his collarbone. This shows that the sage is not some sort of invulnerable super-yogi or something like that, whom nothing can touch. There are invulnerable yogis who develop powers, but they've got huge shields around them. They are not non-dualistic at all. They are very "dual." They say, "Nothing can touch me," but they have invulnerable shields around them. That is super-dualism! That is even more dualistic than the ordinary person. The sage is just open — you might say, loving. In that sense, you could say that he or she is vulnerable. But there is nothing in the sage which could act as the subject of suffering in that sense. So Ramana Maharshi didn't lie on the ground saying "Why me, why me!" when he had his broken collar bone. He just accepted it as the perspectival structure of awareness. He continues:

The universal process of structuring which arises automatically from the perspectival functioning of awareness may appear to be a dream projection by which the Clear Light somehow misleads us into a maze of viewpoints.....

This is funny. Gaudapada's humor is so abstract and refined it is sort of hard to notice it. But this is his way of making a very humorous statement about the "why me" attitude. What if we say, "The Clear Light exists — why don't I have a job?" or "why am I suffering?" or "why am I feeling lost in this world?" Gaudapada says, from the perspectives of awareness it may appear to be that there's a dream projection by which the Clear Light somehow misleads us into a maze of viewpoints. So it is not non-dualism that we are somehow misled into a maze of viewpoints. It is very important to recognize that the non-dualist is not beating his breast and saying, "Woe is me; woe is humanity," or "woe is anything." That "woe, woe, woe" is gone. There are countless viewpoints, but it's not a maze because it doesn't substantiate; it hasn't substantially come into existence. There are no actual walls there. There is nothing but this Panorama of Consciousness regarding which, with great relief, the villager says, "This is just a rope and nothing else." The sage says the same of the universe with all its turmoil, with all its responsibilities — and they are still accepted as responsibilities. Ramana Maharshi felt a responsibility to intervene for the squirrel. Never mind his responsibility for all the human disciples who came to him, he felt as much concern for the squirrel. It was not that the squirrel should be enlightened or practice meditation, but just that it should be saved. Helping turmoil is fundamentally the Open Panorama of Consciousness, and is fundamentally at peace. Gaudapada continues:

This may appear to be a dream projection which the Clear Light somehow misleads us into a maze of viewpoints......

Sometimes, other Vedanta teachers get into this with the doctrine of maya. Gaudapada doesn't really deal with the doctrine of maya. Shankaracharya develops more this doctrine. That we are misled into a maze or something like that is certainly true from a limiting perspective, but Gaudapada speaks from the standpoint of Ultimate Truth — if you could call it a standpoint — in which the very nature of the Open Panorama is Peace. One could say "Love" — it is not meant to be something abstract or cold. It is Reality. All of the vibrancy we see in the earth and in the creation, all this vibrancy, is the nature of Consciousness. So Consciousness is not some sort of static dead thing, nor even like a mathematical formula which may have certain rich implications, while actually being just numbers. You know, these are lives; Consciousness is life. If any teacher says, "This is just a dream projection in which we are being misled into a maze," well, that is a dualistic teacher. Gaudapada goes on:

The Great Affirmations

There is no one who is misled and no process of misleading. There is simply the Panorama of Consciousness.....

In the Upanisads they use the Sanskrit word, *Mahavakya*, "the great affirmation." And that is essentially the way the non-dual Vedanta is passed on: it is expressed. *"There is simply the Panorama of Consciousness."* But one has to prepare oneself to really hear that and to really feel it and make sure that one is not doing a number on oneself or the world by saying "it is just a maze, it is just a dream projection." Everything is very, very real imbued with the reality of Consciousness Itself. One eats, lives, breathes, and moves as the Panorama of Consciousness — not even "in" the Panorama of Consciousness. One might say, "I'm in the Panorama of Consciousness," but that would be dualistic. One would still be some sort of center of consciousness, moving around within the larger consciousness. That doesn't even make sense logically. How could there be different centers of consciousness moving around inside Consciousness? It doesn't make any sense. There is just Consciousness. But Consciousness possesses rich variety in the sense of perspectives.

Gaudapada says that the Panorama of Consciousness is like the pleasure garden, and like the meditation grove: everything is lived as Consciousness. It is proper to say that the sage enjoys, in the sense of the "pleasure garden," the play of perspectives. He or she doesn't look upon it as something nefarious, or something sick or something terrible. He states:

This Open Panorama alone is what appears to project the structures from which thinkers and investigators form speculative or empirical theories about the fundamental nature of existence......

This, of course, applies to physicists and philosophers. But mostly it applies to every human being, because every human being is a thinker and an investigator. Maybe we don't do enough thinking or investigating, but the point is that we all have speculative or empirical theories about our existence.

Gaudapada begins to enumerate this fascinating list of the different kind of speculative or empirical theories that people have developed, mentioning some of the philosophical systems of his time. We should see these as in us too, that is, the seeds of them are in us. For instance, the idea of materialism, that everything comes from matter in motion: most of us might think that it is a kind of inadequate, maybe even absurd theory. Yet we all accept that theory in certain moments of life, in certain moods and certain surroundings. So all of us have these kind of archetypal views of the world. And what Gaudapada is saying is that none of these views of the world are adequate. Let's say there is a civilization in some other galaxy that is so advanced, it's been living for millions of years and has a library with all of the writing that the civilization has ever had, and the most brilliant being among them has come up with a theory of what the universe is. Gaudapada would say no!

Neti neti is a Sanskrit phrase taught in the Upanishads. It means "not this, not this." Na eti — "it's not this." It is kind of a *via negativa*. Someone could say, "What we need is extraterrestrials to come here. Think of the wisdom they would have! Think of the knowledge they have! They can really tell us what it is all about." Gaudapada would smile about this. Nobody can come and give a theory about what it is all about which would be any more than a theory, a perspective. And what he is trying to say is, let's wake up out of all of these perspectives as the Conscious Reality Itself, and then let the perspectives have their play and have their day.

Good, Bad, and Mixed Perspectives

Some perspectives are extremely dangerous. One always thinks of the holocaust — we can't get it out of our minds, which is probably very good. That was a perspective which was vicious and dangerous in the extreme. And there are perspectives which are very, very helpful. Gaudapada says that certain doctrines of the creation in the Upanisads, although he doesn't agree with them as fundamentally the Ultimate Truth, could be helpful to lead us towards a non-dual understanding. The world is sort of like sparks of fire from fire, yes?

At the very early part of these discussions a few months ago, I wanted to make clear to people that there can be mistakes. There can be mistakes in perspectives; that is all. We're not just saying, "It is all fine — all perspectives are equally unreal," or whatever. The scriptures themselves give this example: if you press your eye, you might see two moons. But you can't say, "I live in a universe where there are two moons." Why would you want to live in a universe where there are two moons? Come on! So this could be applied to moral questions too. Mother Teresa obviously has correct moral perspectives, and various oppressive tyrants have demonstrably false perspectives.

So the whole idea of saying, "You can't make any value judgments" goes out the window. Of course there is value judgment. Ramana Maharshi was making a value judgment when he saved that squirrel. It wasn't an intellectual thing, it was a spontaneous act coming from his sense of oneness. Mother Teresa is doing what she's doing spontaneously because of her sense of oneness, but nonetheless it's a true judgment. One time, a reporter asked her whether she believed in war or not. She said, "Absolutely not." And the reporter said, "But the Pope has condoned war. He has given permission for it." She said, "In that case, I'm not a Roman Catholic." [laughter] But she's pure Roman Catholic! She is far more Roman Catholic than the Pope is! The point is that she's unwilling to condone or dignify any false perspective. She's a direct, intuitive person. The sage is that way, and that's why Ramana Maharshi threw his staff. It was a direct, intuitive movement. He didn't step back and say, "Well, the squirrel's karma… the dog's karma…" or, "my karma is just to watch."

I'm still not happy with the term non-dualism, although it is the correct Sanskrit term. Our term unitive vision does not preclude all sorts of sensitive value judgments or intellectual judgments. Gaudapada himself points out the fallacy of the reasoning of certain people. You can't point out a fallacy of reasoning without having a form of reasoning yourself. Let's continue:

As with the rope at twilight, the Panorama of Consciousness is perceived or conceived through various perspectives as the play of the five physical elements…..

Okay, here's a kind of materialism. This kind of materialism did exist in the India of Gaudapada's day. The five elements were called vakas. There was a whole school of very sophisticated thinkers who were aware of the Vedas and Hindu culture, but opted for materialism because they thought it made sense.

There is the other side of the thing as well, that being spiritualists who think that the universe is the play of very subtle energies. The whole yoga school today in the West can be skewed that way too; it may become subtle materialism. But Gaudapada would say both of these "plays" are just perspectives. There is a play of the five physical elements, he is not denying that. There is a play of invisible subtle energy; he is not denying that. What he is saying is that these are just perspectives. What are they perspectives of? What is it ultimately? It's this that he calls the Open Panorama. This is not saying God! This is saying the Open Panorama. God is some sort of magnificent, incredibly rich, powerful perspective, which has the ability to heal and uplift humanity.

But ultimately, what is God? Great mystics do face that ultimate question. They are tremendously devoted to God, but ultimately they get close enough that they really ask. And at that point they don't author philosophies anymore. So we don't know exactly what happens. But we think that it is something like Gaudapada — they awaken as the Open Panorama of Consciousness. But from that standpoint maybe they could say, if they were Christian, "I was illumined by the Holy Trinity." They will experience awakening in that way. I don't think that Vedanta is the future religion of the world in that sense; that eventually everyone will be sitting around with this text, and will dispense with churches and synagogues, and will just have this wonderful over-arching religion or philosophy. I don't think that this is the way it works. I think all of the perspectives remain in play. And a devout Jew, a devout Muslim, a devout Christian, a devout Buddhist, have a very rich variety of perspectives, each of which are just as valid, once one clears out the false judgments. It's the job of religions to purify themselves. It is the job of saints and theologians and devout people to purify the religion of errors and false things that have crept in, whatever the religious tradition may be.

Q: "Earlier, you said that if it is true, one should be able to put it into words. But now you're sort of saying that people have a vision of God and just stop talking."

Gaudapada does put it into words. I think that putting it into words could even be like saying "Neti, neti" — it's not this, it's not this. By "putting it into words," I didn't necessarily mean giving a brute objective description of it, like, "It's round," or "It's empty," or anything like that. Thank you for the question and the clarification. What I mean is that we should be able to articulate very clearly, even where words stop, where the boundary is beyond which words can't go. But it still should be articulated very clearly. Seeing it shouldn't just be a matter of feeling good or being in a high state of consciousness. It is more like a kind of real clarity about the situation.

Many specific philosophies have something of that clarity, but then they become dominant. I mean, if you talk to a Buddhist, a very good well-trained Tibetan Buddhist trained in debate, he will have a crystal clear view — the "correct" view. And it's the "correct" view, believe me. Buddhists are not saying everyone's view is all right. For them, Buddhism is the correct view, and nothing else — everything else might move in that direction, but only Buddhism is the correct view. So, it's wrong to say that so-called Western traditions are exclusive, and in the East, it's all mellow and everything blends. It is not true. The point is that we have to try to get even deeper than these crystalline, correct views of different religious traditions or different philosophies. For instance, modern social sciences have fooled people into thinking that they have a crystal clear view of exactly why people are religious or not religious — because of the structures of their society and the structures of their family. This is like one of the things that Gaudapada is listing:

The Panorama of Consciousness is perceived or conceived through various perspectives as the play of the five physical elements, as the play of invisible subtle energy, as coming from being or from non-being, as states of human awareness or as divine beings in heavenly realms, as the world pictured by revealed scriptures or a field of complex sacred ritual. The same Open Panorama appears to various thinkers to be fundamentally intangible or tangible, discarnate or incarnate or as the space time receptacle of all worlds….

— that's a modern physicist who somehow found himself back in Gaudapada's time and held that view!

To some It appears as a logical system, to others as the mind of the investigator…..

Gaudapada never said that the world was just our mind — never. That is, technically speaking, a kind of philosophical idealism or objectivism. Gaudapada never indulged in that kind of thing. *"To some, it appears as a logical system, to others as the mind of the investigator"* Sometimes physics moves a little in that direction — toward the idea that the mind of the investigator creates the phenomenon. A branch of modern physics has that tendency. Gaudapada goes on:

To some It appears as transcendent intuition, to others as empirical memory. To some, the Panorama of Conscious appears as composed of right and wrong actions….

— "….composed of right and wrong actions." This is the moralistic person — not in a bad sense of "moralistic," but the

> "The Zen Masters say that if you cannot express your realization in words, then you have not had realization."

person who holds the view that right and wrong actions are everything.

— or, it is described as a precise number of metaphysical categories....

This is done in the Sankhya philosophy in India. In Sankhya, there are 24 cosmic principles — exactly, you know, not 23. This type of thing was also done by Emmanuel Kant who, through transcendental analysis and very profound thinking, said that there were ten categories of "the understanding" — such as cause and effect, substantiality, and all that. He said that through these categories we kind of structure our world. But he said there were ten — only ten — not nine, not eleven. He convinced himself absolutely, logically, that this was the case. Gaudapada is not saying that this is bad and no one should be a Kantian, that Emanuel Kant has nothing to say. No, Emmanuel Kant has a lot to say to us. Gaudapada is just saying that to some people Reality appears as composed of right or wrong actions, or it is described as a precise number of metaphysical categories. In Western and Eastern culture there are various systems where Reality is described as a precise number of metaphysical categories. He continues:

To others, the Open Panorama appears as various species of living beings, as stages of human development....

This is Gaudapada 100's of years ago, talking about different disciplines like biology or psychology! This is the biologist and the student of life sciences looking at the various species of living beings. This is the way they see. And it is not wrong. It's like this: I see that this is a pink or salmon-colored flower. That's not wrong. But I have to observe. At first, I was going to call it "pink," which was wrong. I had to connect with the right language and all that. But it doesn't mean that the Panorama of Consciousness is a salmon flower. Unless you want to say it like a Zen master does. You could say "The Buddha is the cypress tree in the garden." We just heard a Zen talk on this the other day. They are saying it in a playful way, to indicate exactly what Gaudapada is indicating in a more philosophical way. Next:

To some the Panorama of Consciousness appears as a precise number of metaphysical categories....

Remember, these are not just ancient systems. This is us, and our existential life as we are walking around the city. We are engaging in these various theories. Further:

To others, the Open Panorama appears as various species of living beings, as stages of human development....

So Maslow was operating fifteen centuries ago, in Gaudapada's time!

....as masculine, feminine, and genderless, or as what is higher and what is lower....

This last one I just want to comment on briefly. People on so-called spiritual quests have got a real bug about this "higher and lower." I must admit I was totally into it, and probably instinctively still am into it, but it has to go. To say that God is higher than his creation, to say that a sage is higher than a person working in McDonald's over there — this is simply not acceptable to the sage. It's not the non-dualistic view to say that the person who chants Krishna's name thousands of times a day is higher than the person who just goes to work on Wall Street. As the sage states next:

Our transmission of wisdom teaches that all these perspectives and all these perceptions and conceptions....

— Those are blended; perception and conception are just two sides of the same thing. We never have an isolated perception or an isolated conception. It is always perceptions-and-conceptions. This is what the perspectives of awareness are made of.

....are simply structures or perspectives of awareness and do not constitute the true nature of the Clear Light of Consciousness....

Perspectival Liberation

At this moment we should all be liberated. I think it does have an impact on us. We are realistic that we have a long way to go, but just to be able to hear this and really accept it transmits an impact.

One could ask, what does constitute the true nature of Consciousness? But that's not really a valid question, because when you have questions, you have perceptions, conceptions, subjects, and objects. However, the valid answer, if you want to call it that, is that It's constituted by the sage who wakes up from identifying with all these perspectives as the Clear Light of Consciousness. And we are the Clear Light of Consciousness.

This Clear Light doesn't have to be forced into us gradually or something like that. We don't have to be refined. Consciousness is not somehow impure. We don't have to gradually wash ourselves like the man who gave the illustration of the different sewage treatments ending up with pure water. All of these are dualistic conceptions which are not ultimately adequate. The rope lying across the path does not have to slowly change from a snake into a rope. It never was a snake!

We are this Clear Light of Consciousness. Even terrible criminals — their actions being totally reprehensible and totally awful — are still the Clear Light of Consciousness. We are nothing but that Clear Light. This is one of Vedanta's great points. Vivekananda used to make this point so strongly — that you are that Infinite Consciousness. Therefore we can have confidence that yes, we could awaken as this. As finite beings we don't have to somehow climb up a steep cliff to attain some infinite state. It would be hard to climb up a steep cliff a couple hundred feet high, but this would be like climbing up an infinitely high cliff. You could never reach it unless you were there already.

When Gaudapada says that all perceptions and conceptions are perspectives of awareness, and that they do not constitute the true nature of the Clear Light of Consciousness, at that moment it should ring a bell. I'd like to just sit for a few moments in silence with this in mind.

The Clear Light is perfectly transparent and perfectly at peace. The Clear Light of Consciousness is appearing absolutely as clearly and fully as every one of the beautiful little black dots on these flowers. You know, actually, these flowers are made out of paper — more and more correction on perspective. But the Clear Light is radiantly appearing through the perspective of black dots on a paper flower.

In this case, I don't feel I have to water this plant, right? Because it is made of paper — that's an appropriate perspective. If I hear someone out there who was hurt and crying, I run downstairs immediately to try to help them. That's also appropriate. There is a great appropriateness in our spontaneous response. The more we awaken as this Clear Light, the more appropriate our actions seem to become, spontaneously without thinking about it. Because there is no way you could really think about everything. So we should sit and contemplate this.

The Ever-Revealed Nature of the Open Panorama

Please don't feel that our true nature is hidden. It is absolutely revealed. One might close one's eyes and have a vision of heavenly realms. Those exist also just as much as Broadway does; they are perspectives. And the sage, which is humanity, which is all of us, can move very freely, in a comfortable manner, between heaven and hell. As Vivekananda would say, "I would be reborn a thousand times if I could just awaken one soul." Because he was irreversibly awake as the Clear Light of Consciousness, he wasn't concerned about being in or out of any world of those perspectives. At one time Vivekananda wanted to get out of this world. He told his master, *"I would like to go into nirvikalpa samadhi and not even have to look at this world, except maybe every three days to drink a little milk and keep the body alive."* A very exalted view, really. But his master took him over the edge, saying, *"You fool, I'll show you a higher state than that."* Then he sang a Sufi hymn, a song saying, *"Everywhere I look I only see Thou. Thou art all that exists."* Sufism is very non-dualistic, with its own way of expressing it.

Q: "Could I say that Light contains everything?"

No, absolutely not — because then it would be a container. Thank you for making that suggestion, though. Our meditation is not like spacing out or blissing out. It consists of continuously correcting limited perspectives that come in and confuse alertness. We definitely couldn't say that the Pure Light contains anything. Gaudapada says that things or substances don't really come into being in the first place. We've been struggling for months to really understand what this means.

In other parts of the *Gaudapadakarika*, he says that Consciousness Itself is not composed of states of consciousness. In fact right here it says, *"Sometimes the Panorama of Consciousness appears as coming from being or from non-being as states of human awareness or as divine beings in infinite realms."* These are just perspectives. States of consciousness are just perspectives. The Clear Light, the Open Panorama is not composed of states of consciousness. It is not composed of matter. It is not composed of consciousness, as if consciousness were some sort of energy or thing. It is Clear Light. You see, we're coming up against total freedom, total liberation if you want to put it that way. But for the non-dualist, there is nothing to be liberated from in that sense. There is nothing other than the Clear Light of Consciousness. So we don't have to say, "Oh I'm stuck in this little cage of flesh, in this little world, and I need to get out of here into the Clear Light of Consciousness." No, there's only the Clear Light of Consciousness.

The world of perspectives is renegotiated constantly by all beings on different levels — for example, culturally — and among different species. Bees perceive things with thousand-faceted eyes and they can operate well in the world. They can tell each other where a flower is by doing a little bee-dance. They create perspectives in their world which are very different from the perspectives of our world.

One could say: "There must be some basic substance upon which the universe is founded." Isn't there at least an invisible subtle energy there that you are kind of structuring? Gaudapada says no. He would say even the word "there" would have to be dispensed with. Where is "there?" It's a perspective. But this is not meant to be kind of a nihilism that sort of takes everything away from us, as we're saying, "Oh my God, what am I going to hold on to? I am going crazy!" It is not meant to be that way. It is meant to free us to move responsibly through these different perspectives. This is meant to be a great spiritual freedom, the kind of spiritual freedom that Christianity taught for instance. Jesus taught a freedom from the restrictions of Jewish law. He said, *"I never came to destroy the law, but to fulfill the law."* He was not ruling out any of these perspectives, but he was teaching a kind of freedom from them. He said that the Sabbath belongs to man, that man doesn't belong to the Sabbath.

So these perspectives belong to us, we don't belong to them. We're talking about freedom even from a basic metaphysical conception like, "What really exists is, well, a big blob of matter"; or "a big blob of energy"; or "God." Well, couldn't we say that Gaudapada is saying "What really exists is Clear Light?" But he's only saying that metaphorically. It's the Open Panorama, and all the value and all of the richness and intensity that we experience as life is the nature of that Open Panorama.

The Open Panorama is not an abstraction. It's not like the mathematical concept zero or something. That's why the sage experiences great delight. People in the presence of the sage experience a light. They feel their problems and their hassles lightening. Then, they can go back to their responsibilities with greater strength, greater commitment. Such is the Open Panorama of Consciousness.

Lex Hixon received his Ph.D. in World Religions from Columbia University in 1976. From about 1971 to the late 80's he conducted a weekly radio show in New York City called "In The Spirit," (ITS) interviewing spiritual teachers from around the world. In the years that followed he entered into deep, serious study and practice of several of the world's religious traditions, eventually becoming a masterful teacher in some of them — including the western chapter of the Jerrahi Order of Istanbul with its several tekkas. Among his books are *Great Swan, Mother of the Universe, Heart of the Koran, Atom from the Sun of Knowledge, Mother of the Buddhas,* and *Living Buddha Zen.* For more information inquire at: **www.lexhixon.org** For ITS Series information inquire at: **www.srv.org**

Swami Brahmeshananda

JAIN MONASTICISM

An Ancient Tradition Defying the Onslaught of a Modern Age

In the tenth article of this long-running series on the noble religion of the Jains, the honorable institution of monasticism is explored, with emphasis on its stages, requirements, mainstays, and challenges.

JAINISM is pre-eminently a monastically oriented religion. According to Jain philosophy, the goal of human life is moksha, liberation from the transmigratory cycle of births and deaths. Perverted views, non-restraint, carelessness, passions, and activity are the five causes of bondage, and these can be totally eliminated by the rigorous practice of a discipline possible only to the monk. So great is the emphasis laid on monasticism, that to renounce the world and to become a monk is one of the prime aspirations of every Jain lay devotee. The Jain luminary, Kumar, goes to the extent of saying that Jainism is simply a monastic organization, an order of begging friars somewhat similar to Dominicans or Franciscans in medieval Europe. Also, the Jain religion is purely an ethical system arising out of its monasticism.

Origin

There are various theories regarding the origin of Jain monasticism. According to orthodox belief, Jainism is eternal. The various similarities between the three monastic systems which have arisen in India — Upanisadic, Buddhistic and Jain — have led some scholars to believe that Jainism was an offshoot or degeneration of Upanisadic concepts. But leading Indologists have conclusively proved that Jainism was a system older than and independent of the two other schools. Jacobi and Garbe consider Jainism and Buddhism as the Kshatriya protest against the class exclusiveness and ritualism of Brahmanism. Others opine that Sramanism (Sramana, wandering mendicant) originated out of the blending of the concept of a celibate, disciplined and studious Brahmacarin, and the Upanisadic concept of Brahmavadin. A Sramana behaves like the former and thinks like the later. To Jacobi, the Jain monastic rules appear to be exact copies of the fourth Ashrama, i.e Sannyasa of Brahmanism. Dutta and Upadhye think that Sramanism developed out of the non-Aryan eastern Indian indigenous elements which did not see eye to eye with the western Aryans who were not very favorable to monastic life. These streams of thought are sometimes termed Magadhan religions. It seems probable that the great wandering communities of Sramanas, with the Jain monastic order as their heart, arose out of blending all these elements.

Historical background

The founders of Jainism and its four branches — monks, nuns, men lay-devotees and women lay-devotees — are the twenty-four Tirthankaras, the first and the last of these being Rsabha and Mahavira respectively. All these prophets were monks and, except Malli, who was a woman, all were men. Only the last two, Parsva and Mahavira, are historical. Parsva was born 250 years before Mahavira, and his order was prevalent when the latter was born. Parsva preached a fourfold religion consisting of non-violence, truth, non-stealing, and non-possessiveness, and allowed monks to wear clothes.

Jainism as practised today is largely based upon the teachings of Mahavira who died in 527 BC at the age of 72. He was succeeded as the head of the Order by Gautama and Sudharma successively. Eight schisms occurred in Jainism, two during the lifetime of Mahavira himself. The final division into the Digambara and Svetambara sects occurred most probably at the end of the first century AD. During the twelve-year long famine in North and West India, a portion of the community migrated to South India. Years later, when the leaders met, it was found that irreconcilable differences (specially regarding nudity) in their modes of living and conduct had developed between them.

Eligibility for Monastic Life

Jain monastic life is open to all, irrespective of caste, status and sex. However, to maintain a high moral standard, and for practical reasons, certain qualifications and restrictions were imposed at a later date. Twenty categories of persons, including some of the following, are debarred from monastic life: a child under eight years, an old person, a eunuch, a sick person, one devoid of limbs, a timid person, and a mad or imbecilic person. Robbers, traitors, enemies of the state, slaves, servants, and persons in debt, were debarred for purely social reasons.

Causes for Renunciation

The majority of people renounce due to disgust for the world and a desire for liberation (*samsarabhaya-udvigna*). Sometimes a woman may renounce when her husband or her son becomes a monk. Some embrace the monastic life after being impressed by the teachings of Mahavira. Besides these, the Jain scriptures cite many worthy and unworthy causes such as anger, poverty, enlightenment in dream, illness, and humiliation, which may lead one to become a monk.

The Ceremony

Irrespective of the motive, the ceremony of initiation (*diksa*) is carried out with full gravity and seriousness. The ceremony is accompanied by great pomp proportional to the social status of the candidate. Particulars of the ceremony vary from sect to sect. In Digambaras, the aspirant stands before the Acarya bereft of all

> "Jainism recognizes as living beings not only those having one to five sense-organs, but also the elemental bodies (sthavara) in the air, water, fire and in earth. A monk is expected to observe ahimsa towards even these categories of living beings."

possessions including the loincloth. He is given a water-pot (*kamandalu*) and a broom (*rajoharana*) made of peacock-feathers to gently remove insects. Among the Svetambars, the aspirant is given three pieces of cloth, a rajoharana or a broom made of woollen tufts, a begging bowl, a blanket, a staff, and some volumes of scriptures. In the Sthanakavasi sect, a strip of cloth to cover the mouth is also given. All these paraphernalia make it easy to identify the monk's sect. It also helps the monk to keep the Mahavratas [described below].

A unique feature of the ceremony is *kesa-loca*, i.e plucking out hair from one's own head and beard. It is said to have been performed by Mahavira, and symbolizes the monk's determination to meet the severe demands of ascetic life. This is repeated every four or six months throughout the monk's life.

Mahavratas

The acceptance of the *Mahavratas*, "Five Great Vows," is common to all the sects of Jainism and forms the most important part of the ordination ceremony. The five vows are:

(1) Ahimsa. Abstaining from injury to all living beings, small or large, moving or stationary. For the perfect practice of this vow the monk must be careful in his movements, thoughts, words, and the upkeep of his belongings. Jainism recognizes as living beings not only those having one to five sense-organs, but also the elemental bodies (*sthavara*) in the air, water, fire, and in earth. A monk is expected to observe ahimsa towards even these categories of living beings. So he refrains from such acts as digging, bathing, swimming, wading through water, lighting or extinguishing fire, fanning himself, walking on greenery, or touching a living plant.

(2) Satya. Truthfulness. This vow is fulfilled by speaking only after careful deliberation, and by giving up anger, greed, fear, and mirth, which may lead one to indulge in falsehood.

(3) Asteya. Non-stealing (literally, not taking what is not given). This is carried out by begging, by asking permission of the superior before consuming food, and by asking permission for staying at a location for oneself and for one's fellow-monks.

(4) Brahmacharya. Abstaining from sexual intercourse. This is carried out by refraining from talking about, looking at, or thinking of members of the opposite sex; by not recalling to mind former sexual pleasures; by avoiding too much food, dainty dishes, and beds used by householders or members of the opposite sex.

(5) Aparigraha. Renunciation of all possessions and attachments. This vow is strengthened when the monk refrains from enjoying sense-pleasures.

All these vows are to be practices in "the thrice threefold way," i.e., the monk must not transgress them himself, nor cause somebody else to do so, nor consent to others doing so, either mentally, vocally, or physically.

The *Dasavaikalika Sutra* adds a sixth vow: abstaining from taking the night meal.

These Mahavratas, especially ahimsa, form the basis of Jain monasticism, and have led to the formation of numerous rules, and regulations, as well as exceptions to the rules to deal with unusual situations.

Samitis and Guptis

The practice of ahimsa is strengthened by five *samitis* and three *guptis*. The five samitis prescribe carefulness regarding movement (*irya*), speech (*bhasa*), begging (*esana*), receiving and keeping things (*adana-nikepana*) and excretory function (*utsarga*). The three guptis consist of control of mind, speech, and body. The tenfold religion (*dharma*) of the monk consists of forbearance, modesty, uprightness, truthfulness, purity, restraint, austerity, renunciation, non-attachment, and continence.

Parisaha

Twenty-two *parisahas* pertain to the troubles and hardships a monk is often subjected to, and which he must conquer by patience and forbearance. These include troubles due to hunger and thirst, heat and cold, mosquitoes and flies, nakedness, wandering life, uncomfortable lodgings, illness, insults and abuses, want of things required, etc.

Tapas (Austerities): Internal and External

Tapas forms an important part, not only of the life of a Jain monk, but of all Jain devotees. So great is the stress laid on tapas that it is added to the *triratnas* to form the fourth pillar of Jainism. It is the most important means of rapid elimination of already accumulate karmas (*nirjara*). There are twelve forms of tapas. The six external austerities are fasting, observing rules regarding food, begging, control of palate, mortification of flesh, and living in solitude. Of greater importance, however, are the internal austerities. They are repentance, humility, service to the monks, study, meditation, and indifference towards the body. Each of these has a number of sub-varieties which are described in detail in Jain scriptures.

Daily Routine of a Monk

According to the *Uttaradhyayana Sutra*, a monk is supposed to sleep only three hours at night, and must spend the rest of the time in study or meditation. His daily duties consist of study, meditation, repentance for sins, begging alms, careful inspection of belongings to avoid injury to insects, and confession of faults. Latter canonical texts prescribe the following six obligatory duties (*avasyaka*) for monks; (i) *samayika*, i.e practice of equanimity through meditation, (ii) *caturvimsati stava*, chanting the

> "....a monk is supposed to sleep only three hours at night, and must spend the rest of the time in study or meditation. His daily duties consist of study, meditation, repentance for sins, begging alms, careful inspection of belongings to avoid injury to insects, and confessions of faults."

praise of Tirthankaras, (iii) *vandana*, veneration of senior monks, (iv) *pratikramana*, expiation of sins, (v) *kayotsarga*, standing or sitting in one posture for a length of time, and (vi) *pratyakhyana*, renunciation of certain foods and activities.

Traditionally, the Jain monks lead wandering lives, except during the four months of the rainy season. There are no monasteries but halls (*upasrayas*) are built by lay devotees where monks can temporarily stay. There are elaborate rules and instructions for begging, for the manner of wandering, and for stay. During the two and a half millennia of growth of Jain monasticism, procedures for dealing with various degrees of transgressions and their punishments have been evolved. The Svetambara texts give ten *prayascittas*, or punishments, the mild ones being confession and condemnation. The harder ones include fasting, penance, and shortening of seniority. The severest is expulsion.

Church-Hierarchy

A candidate having accepted the monastic life is put on probation after a preliminary diksa, called *samayika-caritra*. This involves vows to avoid sins and to practise equanimity. Such a probationer is called a *seha*, *samanera*, or *antevasi*. He must prove himself worthy of monastic life and must show implicit obedience to seniors. After a variable period of seven days to six months, he is confirmed (*upasampada*) and given the final vows, the mahavratas.

There is an elder monk, senior either in age or standing as a monk. This seniority is called *paryaya*. The next higher office is upadhyana. His chief duty is to teach the scriptures (*sastras*) to the junior monks. Next higher designation is the *acarya*. He enjoys certain privileges and must be a man of perfect self-control and monastic discipline. He must be endowed with the five *acaras*, viz., *Jnana-acara*, *Virya-acara*, *Chritra-acara*, *Tapa-acara*, and *Darsana-acara*. He stands at the head of a group of monks. Besides guiding and controlling them, he is authorized to initiate and to confirm candidates.

The *Gani* is yet another post. He possesses eightfold ganisampad; ideal conduct, scholarship, physique, intellect, instruction, debate, organization, and monastic discipline.

Units or Church-groups

To facilitate supervision, solidarity, and study of scripture, the Jain monks form different units. *Gana* is the largest unit having common scriptures. It consists of a number of *kulas* headed by an acarya. No one is allowed to change a gana except for special reasons like advance study of a particular scriptural text. *Sambhoga* is yet another formation of a group taking food together. The most important unit, which is even now prevalent, is *gaccha*. It is supposed to mean the following of one acarya. Sometimes it is equated with the gana.

Jain Nuns

Unlike Buddhism, the Jain order of nuns has been a distinct feature of the Jain church from the very beginning. Mahavira had in his congregation a greater number of nuns (nearly 36,000) than monks, and this state prevails even today. Like men, women also renounce for various reasons. Cases of child-widows becoming nuns are not wanting. Generally, the permission of the guardian must be obtained. Even women must do *kesa-loca*.

Nuns are organized under their officers. *Ganini*, *pravartini*, *theri* and *bhikkuni* are the offices in descending order of importance and seniority. A young nun not yet confirmed is called *ksullika*. All the offices of nuns are subordinate to the offices of monks. This subordination is so supreme that a monk of three year's standing could become the *upadhyaya* of a nun of thirty years' standing.

Like monks, nuns too lead a wandering life, and their rules and regulations are similar to those of monks. A spotless life and practice of rigorous discipline are expected, and punishments for transgressions are severe. Monks and nuns are not allowed to stay under the same shelter, except during calamities or under unforseen circumstances. There are some special rules which help to maintain a pure and unharrassed life of nuns in the society.

Conclusion

One of the noteworthy features of Jainism is the close link which exists between its lay and monastic communities. Jains as a whole are proud of the austere life-style of their mendicants. The solidarity of the Jain social structure too depends to a large extent upon the great moral authority exercised by their austere monks and nuns. The moral decline of the holy men, therefore, becomes a cause of concern for the whole society. Under such situations, the learned among the laity are free to point out the imperfections in the conduct of even the monks. It is noteworthy that some of the important reform movements in Jainism were initiated by enlightened lay-devotees.

There are approximately 8,000 Jain monks and nuns in India today, belonging to some twenty-five different sects. Of the various non-Vedic Sramana traditions, Jainism alone has survived in India until today against heavy odds. This speaks volumes for its vitality and adaptability.

Rules and Exceptions

An important aspect of monasticism is the problem of rules of basic precepts and exceptions to those rules which invariably arise in the process of growth and expansion.

Being a monastically oriented religion, Jainism lays great stress on right conduct. Jain scriptures are overloaded with the finest details around right conduct, rules and regulations, possible pitfalls and penance for default. The principal scriptures, the *angas*, said to be the teachings of Vardhaman Mahavir as recorded by his apostles, describe the basic tenets and fundamental precepts of conduct.

The third section of the second part of *Acaranga Sutra*, (acara-conduct), the most important among the angas, describes the five great vows (mahavratas) with their twenty-five clauses, which are the bedrock of the mighty and complicated edifice of monastic rules. The *Uttaradhyayana Sutra*, which is considered the last sermon of Mahavir, contains more rules and regulations, the restrictions (guptis) and precautions (samitis) which help monks keep their vows. All the rules and sub-rules regarding food, clothing etc., were meant for the perfect and unbroken observance of the mahavratas, with special emphasis on ahimsa or non-violence.

> "There are approximately 8,000 Jain monks and nuns in India today, belonging to some twenty-five different sects. Of the various non-Vedic Sramana traditions, Jainism alone has survived in India until today against heavy odds."

Later Modifications in Rules

Jain monastic rules in their pristine pure form are extremely rigorous. Only a few monks dare to observe them to the letter. These uncompromising ascetics are called *Jinakalpas*. They believe that the written word of the Tirthankar Mahavir must be honored and followed to the letter, and that there is no scope in them for interpretation or explanation. They, however, forget that it is not a question of lack of faith in and disregard for the written word of the Founder, but the ability of the follower to practice them. The majority of aspirants, although possessing complete faith, and having a sincere desire and true aspiration to follow the path, are not sufficiently competent, physically or psychologically, for the most austere way of a literal observance of the law. Out of untempered zeal, if they were to practise the rigorous discipline, they may break down physically or mentally and incur more harm than good. The later Acharyas, who had vast knowledge and lifelong experience of the problems of spiritual life and the complexities of human nature, therefore proposed certain exceptions which were of an almost permanent nature. This led to the development of alternative modes of monastic life. Those who adopted the less rigorous path were called *Sthavirakalpas*. In contrast to Jinakalpa or the solitary mendicant, the Sthavirakalpas lived in a community. Here we see an exception to the original rule itself becoming a rule. The acceptance of garments in place of nudity, as done by the svetambara sect, is the best example of this. Originally done for protection against cold and for social reasons, this exception led to the branching out of a major sect.

Modifications in Rules in the Post-Canonical Period

As the monastic order spread and began to play its social role, the leaders of the monastic community were faced with the conflict between upholding the original tenets on the one hand, and the need to preserve the prestige and safety of the Sangha on the other. They tried their best to reconcile the spiritual welfare of the individual aspirant with the welfare of the Sangha, but at times they were forced, at the expense of the individual, to relax the rules in order to glorify the Sangha and to ward off danger to the monastic community. In the post-canonical period, when Jainism spread to various parts of India, monks were allowed to deviate from general rules according to place, time, and situation. They resorted to magical practices and spells to demonstrate their prowess to kings, whose goodwill mattered for the survival of the Jain community. They even entered into politics and dethroned kings if it was profitable for the Jain community. Monks had to organize religious congregations and engage themselves in writing books. All these made relaxation of certain rules inevitable. At times, even improper acts were permitted for the sake of the Sangha. Examples may be cited.

A monk was prohibited from inflicting injury to a clay-image of an enemy after infusing life into it with the help of incantations. But he was allowed to do so if the person concerned was an enemy of the Sangha. Once a group of monks had to pass the night in a forest infested with wild beasts. An exceptionally robust monk was deputed as a guard. The monk on duty killed three tigers and saved the Acharya and others. His act, though blatantly against the vow of ahimsa, was not condemned. According to another exception, monks were permitted to take recourse to violence, if need be, to protect nuns.

The general rule for the monk is that he must not touch greenery or step upon grass, since it also contains life, which he has vowed not to injure. But, according to the Acaranga, "the *mendicant might stumble or fall down; when he stumbles or falls down, he can catch ahold of trees, shrubs, plants, creepers, grass or sprouts to extricate himself.*"

It will be observed that in the final analysis, this exception supports ahimsa inasmuch as on falling, the monk may injure other creatures, and on being hurt he may engage in unwholesome thinking related to pain, illness etc. (*raudra* and *arta dhyana*), thus triggering a train of events not conducive to the ultimate goal.

A monk is debarred from leaving the place of residence while it is raining. This is the general rule. But as an exception he may go out in the rain for answering calls of nature. Forceful restraint of calls of nature is harmful for health and leads to mental unrest, which is undesirable.

Let us take another example. Observance of truth is one of the mahavratas. In the *Acaranga*, an exception is described thus: "*While going on a road, if a hunter or some such person with suspicious intention asks the monk whether he has seen any animal or human being around, the monk should first try to evade the answer and keep quiet. But if it is not possible to remain silent, or if silence is likely to be construed as affirmation, then although knowing, he should say that he does not know.*"

Under the vow of non-stealing, monks, as a rule, cannot stay at a place without prior permission. But as an exception, if it is not possible to stay outside or in a forest, and if the monks reach an unknown village at night, they may stay at a suitable place at night and seek permission later. A monk, vowed to practice chastity in thought, word, and deed, must not touch even a newly born female child. But there is this exception: he can catch hold of a drowning nun and pull her out to save her life.

From the above illustrations it is evident that the possibility of exceptions can never be denied, and even the founders of monastic rules were conscious of this fact. It must, however, be noted that these exceptions pertain only to temporary situations. The monk is expected to revert to the practice of basic precepts as soon as the specific situation is over. These are extreme illustrations, but they highlight to what extent changes in basic concepts can occur in the course of history.

Mahavir was prepared to, and actually did, undergo untold suffering inflicted by an enemy, without resisting. But his monastic followers resorted to the common dictum for laymen that an enemy of *Dharma* (*atatayi*) must be punished. It also demonstrates the fact that a stage comes when the welfare of the Sangha and the propagation of the Faith become more important than the personal salvation of the individual. The individual does not then hesitate to do something for the Sangha which he may never do for himself. His act is justified on the ground that the Sangha is essential for the propagation of the only right path. Such acts also suggest the belief that the ends justify the means, as against the basic ethical postulate that means are as important as the ends.

The general precepts must be always followed by all. They cannot be given up permanently, and even when they are bypassed occasionally, there must be valid reasons for doing so. Medicines are used only when there is some ailment, and are discontinued after one is cured. Similarly, if a monk resorts to exceptions under special situations, but does not revert to the rules after the situation is over, he is either insincere or has a wrong concept of rules and exceptions. An aspirant must, therefore, be extremely cautious so that he is not deceived by his subtle desires, which may urge him to take permanent shelter under the exceptions. The minimum possible exception must be made only for the shortest period of time, and that, too, when no other alternative is available, because there is always the danger that one may want to resort indefinitely to exceptions to suit one's convenience. Those who have neither the sense of proportion nor the knowledge of the limitations of exceptions, fall headlong, like a ball rolling down a staircase. For such people, exceptions are never a help, but a hindrance. The real spirit of an exception is well demonstrated in the following story:

During a prolonged famine, a learned monk wandering in search of food came across a group of people sharing a common meal. When he begged for a little food they told him that the food was unfit for consumption by a monk because it was impure (*ucchista*). The monk cited the scriptural exception that during a calamity such restrictions do not apply, and said he would accept the impure food. After eating, however, he refused to drink water, saying that it was impure! He explained that when he had begged for food he was dying of hunger, and there was no immediate possibility of getting pure food approved by scriptures. So he made the exception. But now he was no more dying of hunger and could wait for pure water which could be had elsewhere. Why should he then break the rule for water?

Similar precautions must be observed while relaxing the rules for the welfare of the Sangha. Such relaxations may not prove spiritually detrimental if the spirit of renunciation and total dedication to the fundamentals of monastic life are kept alive. In the absence of these, even the strictest observance of rules may be nothing more than lifeless pretension or mere ostentation.

In spite of such unusual exceptions, the moral conduct and character of the monks on the whole remained good. But it is obvious that such relaxation cannot be conducive to any permanent good. Monks gradually started relaxing rules on the false pretext of serving the Sangha. Overemphasis on catering to the religious needs of lay-devotees led to the entanglement of monks in secular matters. They started living in permanent dwellings (*catiya-vasa*) with their associated ills.

To summarize, the basic rules laid down by the first founders of the Jain monastic order underwent change in a stepwise manner. Initially, the founders themselves postulated some important exceptions for specific situations. The subsequent heads of the Order laid down some exceptions for the larger section of less competent aspirants, which became an alternative but equally valid path for the majority. The next stage was marked by exceptions introduced for the propagation, glorification, and welfare of the monastic order — the Sangha. In the final stage, changes of such magnitude occurred so obviously in the monastic conduct, that a reform was called for. This is not the story of Jain monasticism only, but is true of the monastic communities of other religions too.

A former editor of the Vedanta Keshari, and previously of the Ramakrishna Mission Home of Service, Swami Brahmeshananda is a senior monk of the Ramakrishna Order and until recently was the Secretary of the Ramakrishna Mission Ashrama in Chandigarh, India. Over the years his writings in Hindi and English have appeared in several journals, including Prabuddha Bharata, Vedanta Kesari, and Nectar of Nondual Truth. He specializes in themes related to Jainism. He is now retired and is living in Varanasi.

◆ Annapurna Sarada

≈ svadhyaya ≈
The Benefits of Memorizing Scripture

Before the invention of writing, culture and daily communication was passed on orally and stored in one's memory. Before literacy and access to books was widespread, memorization was an integral part of life. Even with growing literacy and printing presses much was committed to memory. Before cell phones, we memorized the phone numbers and addresses of family and friends. Before the internet, we remembered what book or magazine we had read something in. Today, we are more likely to skim-read whatever we are interested in and expect that if we need that information later, we can Google it with a few search words. Though we have nearly infinite access to all kinds of information on the web, turning it into knowledge requires effort. Information becomes knowledge when we "know" it, which means that we have it at our disposal via memory. Maybe we heard or saw it so many times that it naturally lodged there. Perhaps we consciously memorized it. There are also prodigies who acquire knowledge or an ability at an astonishing speed as if they were only calling it back to memory after just a little introduction. But no matter how we find it, knowledge is always inside, there in the mind. No one can know something for us. Swami Vivekananda writes in Karma Yoga:

Now this knowledge, again, is inherent in man. No knowledge comes from outside; it is all inside. What we say a man "knows," should, in strict psychological language, be what he "discovers" or "unveils"; what a man "learns" is really what he "discovers," by taking the cover off his own soul, which is a mine of infinite knowledge. We say Newton discovered gravitation. Was it sitting anywhere in a corner waiting for him? It was in his own mind; the time came and he found it out. All knowledge that the world has ever received comes from the mind; the infinite library of the universe is in your own mind. The external world is simply the suggestion, the occasion, which sets you to study your own mind, but the object of your study is always your own mind. Complete Works of Vivekananda, vol. 1, p. 28

According to tradition in India, and dating back thousands of years, knowledge is to be revered and is of two kinds: lower knowledge called *aparavidya*, and higher Knowledge called *Paravidya*. Lower knowledge consists of knowledge of the world. In modern times this would be science, mathematics, humanities, the arts, and all vocational skills, hence, knowledge to make one's way in life, hopefully in a spirit of service. Higher knowledge is defined in one of two ways, 1) knowledge leading to Self-Realization, such as scriptures and dharma, or 2) Self-Realization itself. For our purposes here, we will be guided by the first definition. This concept of knowledge — its division as higher and lower as well as the truth that all knowledge is internal, not external — underlies the following discussion of *svadhyaya* because, although svadhyaya pertains specifically to study and memorization of higher knowledge, its practice will be suggestive of how we understand all knowledge. We are accustomed to think that memorization is a practice of stuffing new things into the mind, but the yogic view, as Swami Vivekananda states above, is that the act of memorization causes us to study our own mind and what lies therein at its most subtle levels.

Svadhyaya is commonly known among practitioners of Yoga and Vedanta as one of the five *niyamas* (beneficial practices), the second limb in Patanjali's Eight-Limbed Yoga. It is generally defined as study or recitation of scripture. The other niyamas are austerity, purity, contentment, and self-surrender/worship of God. All five are considered necessary to balance and purify the mind and qualify it for transcendence of the dualities of life such as pain and pleasure, life and death, virtue and vice, etc. Svadhyaya, together with austerity and self-surrender, is considered a special yoga, called *Kriya Yoga*, by Patanjali. Notice how potent this threesome is. Self-surrender to God, from whom all knowledge proceeds, opens the mind via humility and matures the ego that would otherwise limit the flow of knowledge into one's awareness by claiming it as "my knowledge." Austerity, as defined by Sri Krishna, purifies the body, speech, and mind making it possible to concentrate without the ceaseless arising of desires and karmic repercussions. [see chart, The Three Dispositions of Living Beings, on page 37 of this issue of Nectar of Nondual Truth]

Svadhyaya is not merely reading scripture. It implies that one studies each verse carefully, committing it to memory so that one can reflect inwardly upon it at will. One mere reading of a verse is rarely adequate to cause it to stick in the mind of today's modern person, much less allow its deeper significance to be revealed. Svadhyaya assumes that one engages in *manana* (reasoning and contemplation), the second of three proofs of truth: *shravana* (hearing the Truth from an illumined soul), *manana*, and *nididhyasana* (realization). Svadhyaya also means recitation of scripture. This is not to be understood as reading the scriptures aloud from a book. It means reciting verses from memory. This is very different from rote memorization. Rote memorization does not include contemplation. It is empty. One's tongue can be moving and pushing out words while the mind thinks of something else. Svadhyaya means that as one recites the verse, aloud or silently, there is deep communion with its meaning.

"Nonrecitation of the scriptures is the rust of monasteries, nonexertion in spiritual practice is the rust of households; sloth is the rust of all that is truly beautiful; negligence is the rust of the spiritual vigil." – Lord Buddha in the Dhammapada

The primary purpose of this great spiritual discipline of svadhyaya is to lead the mind into the lower samadhis of wisdom and bliss, and high devotional states *(bhavas)*, and finally into *Nirvikalpa Samadhi* — absorption in *Brahman*, which is identical with *Moksha*, Freedom. As Shankara states in verse 364 of the *Vivekachudamani*:

*Om shruteh shata-gunam vidyan mananam mananad api
Nidhidhyasam lakshagunam anantam nirvikalpakam*
"Hearing about Brahman is good. Taking teachings on Brahman [and contemplating them, mananam] is better. Meditating directly on Brahman is better still. But best of all is that meditation in which all doubt about the nature of Reality dies away forever."

Like any spiritual practice, svadhyaya does not directly cause Self-Realization or Moksha, Liberation; for these are the natural condition of the true Self at all times. As Swami Aseshananda often stated, *"Liberation is not the effect of any cause."* But he also repeatedly affirmed that *"....self-effort and Grace go hand in hand,"* echoing Sri Ramakrishna's teaching that *"the wind of God's Grace is ever blowing, but one must raise one's sail to catch it."* Grace may be said to be a devotional way of expressing the Advaitic truth that Existence, Awareness, and Bliss/Freedom is our very nature and ever-present. It is the ultimate healer, protector, inspirer, etc. Thus, the goal of svadhyaya is to set one up to recognize one's ever Pure, ever Awake, ever Free nature. A steady practice of svadhyaya is the self-effort that tunes one's mind to more and more subtle states of awareness. Meditation without the practice of svadhyaya to enliven it, sharpen it, and inspire it, can easily lead to a "blankness" that is more akin to the dullness of tamas than the "Void," which is described as a blissful, luminous state of formlessness.

Svadhyaya unfailingly grants the spiritual practitioner many benefits. Memorization and contemplation of scripture imbues one with a deep understanding of the dharma. Dharma is a broad word. We are using it here in the sense of those teachings that clarify one's doubts about the nature of Reality, the Self, the world, and one's relationship to each, and which empower one to live a divine life of unwavering inner peace. Thus, one can see that not all scriptures will qualify for memorization. Sri Ramakrishna acknowledged that most scriptures are a mixture of sand and sugar, and that the practitioner must be like an ant and take just the sugar. Therefore, when selecting a scripture or particular verses, we can and must be choosy. From the Vedanta, scriptures like the *Upanisads, Bhagavad Gita, Narada's Bhakti Sutras, Vivekachudamani,* devotional hymns that cultivate devotion to *Ishvara,* the Personal God, and nondual hymns glorifying the ever-blissful Self — all these are tried and true, and easily accessible in many languages.

Memorization of these dharma teachings develops concentration, one-pointedness of mind. One may be experiencing a sleepy or monkey-mind meditation, but calling up a verse of scripture and contemplating it awakens the drowsy mind and fuses all the *chitta vrittis,* thought waves of the mind, into one wave of inspired thought. It leads to what is called *tailadhara dhyan,* or meditation that is like the flow of oil from one beaker to another — a steady stream without splashing. Daily recitation and contemplation affects one's mind outside of formal meditation as well. As one's mind becomes more and more imbued with the dharma teachings and has an abundant reserve of them from which to draw, brooding on ordinary, random, negative, or superficial thoughts dwindles away with just a little effort. Why should one let the field of the mind get choked by the weeds of brooding on the past and worrying about the future? Recalling the dharma teachings clears them away like a fresh wind scatters clouds from the vision of the "sun," one's self-effulgent, blissful nature.

Becoming skillful in this use of svadhyaya results in a peaceful mind; for, one is now increasingly preoccupied with what is Eternal and able to recognize and deal appropriately with what is not eternal. This grants forbearance and fortitude in one's daily life. By holy association with the illumined thoughts of the seers and Avatars, one imbibes their detachment from the non-Self and strives to *"Locate the body-bound 'I'-sense in the ever blissful spiritual Self."* (Adhyatma Upanisad) Initially, this will be an intellectual effort founded on reasoning and working out the teachings in one's mind and life, yet it leads ultimately to true insight and spiritual experience (niddidhyasana). *"The mind of the yogin perishes as he stays without intermission in the Self alone, knowing through shruti (revealed scripture), reasoning, and experience, that he is the Self in all beings."* (ibid.)

From the standpoint of Indian spiritual philosophy, purity of mind is readily assessed by one's ability to contemplate God/Soul/Atman without distraction, at will. Sri Ramakrishna often pointed out to his disciples, *"The mind that dwells on these three [property, spouse, money] cannot be fixed on God."* [Gospel of Sri Ramakrishna, p. 739]. Spiritual practitioners often lament that the mind will not settle down for meditation, but goes running off in all directions. When asked why this is, the teacher will reply that it is due to *vashana samskaras,* inherent tendencies from prior lifetimes based in desire for enjoyment of objects and relationships. We might as well explain it as desire for life, for physical experiences. If we spend time contemplating this answer we will see how true it is. The destruction of all samskaras, which occurs through repeated experience of Nirvikalpa Samadhi, is hailed as liberation in life.

Long before such a state is attained, however, samskaras for spiritual life, devotion, intelligence, and dharma are extremely helpful at the beginning, middle, and even advanced stages of spiritual life. Babaji Bob Kindler often stresses that the West needs to develop samskaras for dharma. He compares these to having an inner canyon wall that will echo back to you in successive lifetimes: "Does God exist?" "Exists!" "Should I practice meditation?" "Meditation!" Those with positive samskaras for spiritual life will pick up the thread of their yoga, as Sri Krishna states. And for those who are just opening their eyes to dharma for the first time, *"....even a little practice of this dharma will save one from the great fear"* and will become the basis (i.e., form samskaras for dharma) for picking up the thread of one's yoga in the next lifetime. As Krishna tells Arjuna in this regard, *"O Partha, neither in this world nor in the next is there destruction for him; for, the doer of good never comes to grief. Having attained to the worlds of the righteous and having lived there for countless years, he who falls from yoga is reborn in the house of the pure and prosperous. Or he is born in a family of wise yogis only; a birth like this is verily very difficult to obtain in this world. There he regains the knowledge acquired in his former body, and he strives more than before for perfection. By that very former practice he is led on in spite of himself. Even he who merely wishes to know of yoga rises superior to the performer of rites."*
Sri Krishna, Bhagavad Gita vs. 40 - 44

(continued on page 36)

Wisdom Facets From the Gem of Truth

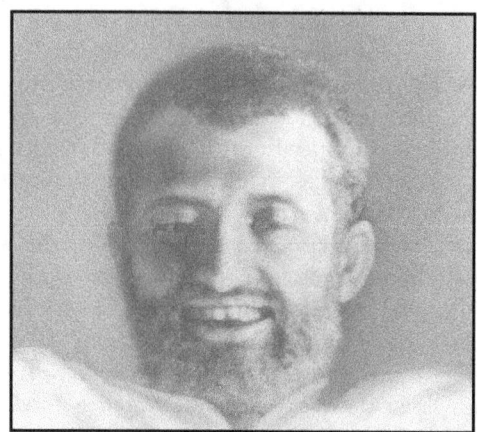

Sri Ramakrishna

Holy Mother, Sri Sarada Devi

The Reality is One and the Same.

"The yogi seeks to realize the Paramatman, the Supreme Soul. His ideal is the union of the embodied soul with the Supreme Soul. He withdraws his mind from sense-objects and tries to concentrate it on the Paramatman. Therefore, during the first stage of his spiritual discipline he retires into solitude and with undivided attention practices meditation in a fixed posture. But the Reality is one and the same. The difference in only in name. He who is Brahman is verily Atman, and again, He is Bhagavan. He is Brahman to the followers of the path of knowledge, Paramatman to the yogis, and Bhagavan to the lovers of God."

(Gospel of Sri Ramakrishna)

"O Mind, Stop Functioning...."

"The upshot of the whole thing is that, no matter what path you follow, yoga is impossible unless the mind becomes quiet. The mind of the yogi is under his control; he is not under the control of his mind. When the mind is quiet the prana stops functioning. Then one gets Kumbhaka. One may have the same Kumbhaka through bhaktiyoga as well: the prana stops functioning through love of God too."

(Gospel of Sri Ramakrishna)

Disciplinary Diplomacy

"One should not discuss the discipline of the Impersonal God or the path of knowledge with a bhakta. Through great effort perhaps he is just cultivating a little devotion. You will injure it if you explain away everything as a mere dream."

(Gospel of Sri Ramakrishna)

Sharp as a Razor's Edge is the Path....

"It is easy to worship God with form. But it is not as easy as all that."

(Gospel of Sri Ramakrishna)

Consciousness alone Abides

"Does anything happen without the will of God? Even a leaf on a tree does not move without His wish. According to His will, this universe and all beings are functioning. Can an object function if there is no consciousness behind it?"

(Sri Sarada Devi and Her Divine Play)

The Secret of Liquified Mind

"The mind becomes pure by discussing the lives of great souls. Look, the movement of water is always downward; but the scorching sun evaporates the ocean water as vapor, which rises up and is blown away by the wind to the top of the mountains. There it becomes snow; then it melts as water, and flows through springs and rivers and helps humankind."

(Sri Sarada Devi and Her Divine Play)

On Raising Children

"One should communicate with children in a simple and intimate way. You should allow them to play with children of their own age. Never scold them too much and never physically abuse them. If you reprimand them severely or beat them, they may be frozen with fear and will run away from you. They will understand easily if you lovingly help them understand. Never refuse to answer their questions by rebuffing them or threatening them. If you scold and intimidate them, they will be afraid to ask questions, which will impede the natural development of their minds."

(Sri Sarada Devi and Her Divine Play)

The Destruction of Karma

"If you want to escape the results of good and bad karma, then chant God's name, repeat your mantra, worship the Lord, and read the scriptures. Always discriminate between the real and the unreal."

(Sri Sarada Devi and Her Divine Play)

Wisdom Facets From the Gem of Truth

Swami Vivekananda   Sri Ramakrishna's Disciples & Devotees

The Two Schools of Spirituality and Materialism
"The issue has to be fought out between the reincarnationists — who hold that all experiences are stored up as tendencies in the subject of those experiences, the individual soul, and are transmitted by reincarnation of that unbroken individuality — and the materialists, who hold that the brain is the subject of all actions and the theory of the transmission through cells. It is thus that the doctrine of reincarnation assumes an infinite importance to our mind, for the fight between reincarnation and mere cellular transmission is, in reality, the fight between spiritualism and materialism."

Real Strength Lies Within, and is Subtle
"We see a man take up a huge weight, we see his muscles swell, and all over his body we see signs of exertion, and we think the muscles are powerful things. But it is the thin threadlike nerves which bring power to the muscles; the moment one of these threads is cut off from reaching the muscles, they are not able to work at all. These tiny nerves bring the power from something still finer, and that again in its turn brings it from something finer still — thought...."

Easy to Say, Hard to Do
"There is a vast difference between saying 'food, food' and eating it, between saying 'water, water' and drinking it. So, by merely repeating the words 'God, God,' we cannot hope to gain realization. We must strive and practice."

Truth or Comfort?
"However comfortable mankind may consider Heaven, truth is one thing and comfort is another. There are cases where even truth is not comfortable until we reach its climax. Human nature is very conservative. It does something, then finds it hard to get out of it. The mind will not receive new thoughts, because they bring discomfort."

All Selections, Complete Works of Vivekananda

Universal Salutations
"Our salutations go to all the past Prophets whose teachings and lives we have inherited, whatever might have been their race, clime, or creed! Our salutations go to all these God-like men and women who are working to help humanity, whatever may be their birth, color, or race. And our salutations to those who are coming in the future — living Gods — to work unselfishly for our descendants."

(Swami Satprakashananda, Hinduism and Christianity)

The Doctrine of Divinity
"If one thinks that the body of the guru is the guru, then the doctrine of the guru will end with the doctrine of the body (dehatmavad). But if one considers the guru as the Ishta, or the Chosen Deity, then when the guru dies, one will not miss the guru. That guru is the eternal guru."

(Swami Bhuteshananda, Sri Sarada Devi and Her Divine Play)

These Three Things....
"Instead of sitting idly by, waiting for an illumined soul to become your guru, make an effort to do these three things which are necessary for spiritual life: contemplate God, study the scriptures, and associate with the holy. First, prepare the ground by digging, removing the weeds, and watering the soil with earnest care. One of the secrets of life, which will be revealed to you if study nature intelligently, is that as soon as the soil is ready the sower of the seeds inevitably comes."

(Swami Saradananda, Glimpses of a Great Soul)

What? Me Worry?
"Man always worries about his future. Undue worry produces restlessness. Avoid worry, and life runs smoothly. Suppose even that the body is to be given up. What does it matter? The Master has shown us that it is nothing."

(Swami Turiyananda, Life and Teachings)

SCRIPTURAL SAYINGS
of the World's Religious Traditions

"Verily, from yoga arises wisdom, and from lack of it the loss of wisdom. Having become aware of this twofold path that leads to progress and decline, let the devotee place himself in such a way that his wisdom increases. And when it does, then he should cut down the entire forest, not just a single tree. Cut down the forest and remove the brush, and become emancipated."

"When nourishment is pure, reflection and higher understanding become pure. When reflection and higher understanding are pure, memory become strong. When memory becomes strong, there is the release of all the knots of the heart. After all impurities are washed off, the seers reveal to sincere seekers the farthest shore beyond all darkness."

"I looked upon all the works that my hands had wrought, and on the labor that I had labored to do; and behold, all was vanity and pursuit of the wind, and there was no profit under the sun. And I turned within myself to behold wisdom, as well as madness and folly. Then I saw that wisdom excelled folly, as far as light excels darkness. Then I invested myself with her as a raiment of glory, and put her on my head as a crown of joy."

"Thou remainest ever the same, and thy years will not change that. For thine soul is not hidden; neither is it far off. It is not in heaven, nor is it beyond the sea. Verily it is nigh unto thee, nestled deeply in thine own heart."

"The moment that this mystery has been unveiled unto thine eyes that thou art no other than Allah, thou shalt know that thou art thine own end and aim, and that thou has never ceased and can never cease to be."

"There is no suitable name for the Tao. And that Tao that can be expressed is not the eternal Tao, the name which can be named is not the eternal Name. The man who knows the Tao does not speak; he who speaks, knows it not. The eternal Tao has no name; when the Tao divided itself, then it had a name."

Babaji Bob Kindler ◆

Householders, Sadhana, & Spirituality
Living a Dharmic Life in the World

Wherever one looks, especially in the West (though most of the world now mimics the West) one glaring lack is evident. In society, at work, in schools, at home, in modern books and movies, if the observer scrutinizes life, even generally, the absence of the performance of spiritual practice is sorely missing. One might just as well say that spiritual life itself has been abandoned by today's societies and their peoples. The result of overlooking this crucial element of life in the world is seen in the gradual breakdown of Western society itself — its moral fabric, its systems of justice, its awareness around environment and food, its compassion for other nations, the deterioration of healthy family life, even the ensuing fragmentation of the individual and collective mind and its very thought process. Thus, externally and internally, the overall well being of America and Europe is undergoing a process of decay reminiscent of the fate of once powerful Western countries of the past. And ironically enough, the one solution for this premature demise is the very thing that the West resists, and will have none of — sadhana, spiritual disciplines and their practice.

The Unholy Matrimony of Materialistic Science and Conventional Religion

Lamentably, what passes for an inner life today is that decrepit, tired, worn-out, institution called conventional religion. Adherents of this poor substitute for authentic devotional life declare, "I am A Jew," "I am a Christian," "I am a Hindu," or claim any other religious affiliation as their own. But they are not real practitioners of the great world traditions; they have only inherited outer religious forms from their ancestors over a few generations. They know neither the meanings of these external rituals nor how to bring any real quality to or out of them, for meaning and quality belong to true Religion, a principle that they know nothing about. Nor do they evince any interest in finding out about it, what to speak of Divine Reality behind it. Their main excuse for this gross oversight is that religion is responsible for all the ills of the world, and thus is a subject unworthy of entertaining.

But that is not what the seers think or say, even ones of recent record. As Swami Vivekananda has stated, *"I claim that no destruction of religion is necessary to improve society, and that this state of society exists not on account of religion, but because religion has not been applied to society as it should have been. This I am ready to prove from our old books, every word of it."* With convincing fervor, the enlightened Swami continues, citing the reasons why religion has lost its worth for the Westerner: *"India's religion should be preached in Europe and America. Modern science has undermined the basis of religions like Christianity. Over and above that, luxury is about to kill the religious instinct itself."*

Comfort and science, then, the dual preoccupation of the Western mind, are potential threats to a healthy and ardent spiritual life. Really, one can hardly separate them, or even find any marked difference in them nowadays. The desire to formulate a utopian society (the very attainment being rather a contradiction in terms) has been the West's greatest desire for centuries, and has led it to a preoccupation with power — either of the material kind or of the occult variety. Seeing this strong tendency upon his arrival in America and England in the 1890s, Vivekananda made some startling and quite telling observations about the West in this regard: *"Nowhere have I heard so much about 'love, life, and liberty' as in this country, but nowhere are they less understood. Here God is either a terror, or a healing power, a vibration, and so forth. Lord bless their souls. And these parrots talk day and night of love, and love, and love. But the West is a nation of mammon-worshipers. Money comes before everything. People of India are very liberal in pecuniary matters, but not so much these people. Every home has a miser. It is almost a religion here. But they fall into the clutches of the priests when they do something bad, and then buy their way to heaven with money. These things are the same in every country — priestcraft."*

So, as if pleasure and scientific knowledge were not enough of an unsavory amalgam, the way is left open for conventional religion to enter the fray. Ironically, religion and science were ever at loggerheads since the birth of this nation, yet here they are, together and in cahoots around money and materialism. This is why the seers prescribe to Truth-seekers that echelon of Awareness called spirituality, and mark its distinct nature.

Acknowledging the Problem, Seeking the Solution, and Staying the Path

If the problem of the unholy trinity of materialistic science, fundamentalist religion, and a hedonistic and pleasure-loving society is admitted by modern humanity, and the cure of true Religion can be agreed upon and firmly resorted to, then the panacea of a complete reworking of the human mind on a deep level can be administered. This will necessarily end up in the hands of what the ancient seers have termed *sadhana*, defined as self-effort, spiritual practice, inner life, *dharma*, etc. Where this regimen of practice is adhered to there is to be found peace of mind and right thinking. Where it is absent, there one sees, in time, the deterioration of society at all its fundamental levels.

To begin on the inward journey once again, the people of

modern times will have to disassociate religion from all its false associations of the past, and from those purblind individuals and organizations who have constructed and fostered them. Swami Vivekananda, who brought us a drought of fresh water and a breath of fresh air in this recent time, spiritually speaking, has put it this way: *"This is a thoroughly materialistic country. The people of this Christian land will recognize religion if only you can cure diseases, work miracles, and open up avenues to money, and understand little of anything else. All these old, foggy forms are mere superstitions. Why struggle to keep them alive? Why give thirsty people dirty ditch-water to drink whilst the river of life and truth flows by?"*

the value of the dharma, or put conversely, realizes that the absence of dharma will eventually result in the advent of confusion leading to chaos — the breakdown of a Godless society. For, as the seers would have it, *"To be good and to do good — that is the whole of religion."* And if we be truly Christian, we must act on the dictum of *"Not he that crieth 'Lord, Lord,' but he that doeth the will of the Father."*

The Secret of True Religion

Whereas much more could be said about the ills and cautionary measures around these three usurpers, the actual imple-

> "Jnanam, as Indian traditions call her, which is unsurpassed for bringing about higher understanding leading to direct spiritual experience, has to be held sacrosanct. It is not so much that it is to be kept on an ivory throne; it *is* the ivory throne. Reverence for it as a sentient principle must be engendered by humanity."

To transform this information into a plan, first, we are not to allow occult movements and their machinations to masquerade for true Religion. The occult has its own realm, as dreamlike a play as life on earth, and all who are attracted there are welcome to it. But it cannot compete nor compare with true Religion — neither in quality nor in profundity.

Secondly, healing is not to be mistaken for matters of the Spirit, since it applies to the physical, mainly, and to the flow of gross and subtle energy and their impedance. Where healing of the mind, intellect, and ego are concerned, that is the realm of psychology, and in that realm we are to inquire after the traditions of the East for their wisdom methods and apt conclusions. Why? Because after 2000 years of so-called Western religion, wherein we have hardly seen any real and true progress in the areas of crucial spiritual subjects such as inner cosmology (not outer space, but inner space), living philosophy (free of mere argumentation), conscious reincarnation (which proves that bodies are without number, but the Soul is One), and transcendence of suffering — what to speak of meditation, nondual wisdom, and samadhi, and the realization of the divine nature of our own innate Awareness — it is far past time to beg, borrow, or even plead for higher understanding to be given regarding these crucial principles. For the mind's health, then, the authentic eight-limbed Yoga must be taught and practiced.

Third, that old poisonous tendency of using religion to open "avenues to money" has to be curtailed. In this world, money can hardly be disallowed in any undertaking, religion included. What must be avoided, however, is accepting money for teaching spiritual wisdom — to anyone, rich and poor alike. Jnanam, as Indian traditions call her, which is unsurpassed for bringing about higher understanding leading to direct spiritual experience, has to be held sacrosanct. It is not so much that it is to be kept on an ivory throne; it *is* the ivory throne. Reverence for it as a sentient principle must be engendered by humanity. As for finance in religion, funds for keeping religion's salutary aims current and in step with human need can be accomplished via the time-honored way of pious donations from a society that realizes

mentation of sadhana into daily life gets more at the solution. Sadhana is all that the seers have said about it, all that it has been chalked up to be. When consistently and systematically applied to the problems of life and the limitations of the mind it will end the chimerical game of human ignorance and bring down the final curtain on the saga of human suffering. But it must be well-guided and adhered to with constancy.

Sadhana is not something that is utilized to remove inconsistencies and impurities, only to be cast aside later as unneeded. Since it is the nature of this world to produce and present all manner of distraction, and the nature of mind to contain and concoct all the vagaries and vicissitudes of life, then spiritual self-effort must be ongoing. And in order for it to be so, the aspiring soul must build a spiritual life in which faith plays an important role. All the great luminaries have possessed this quality of faith. As Swami Vivekananda said, *"I have never lost faith in a benign Providence, nor am I going ever to lose it; my faith in true Religion and scriptures is unshaken."* When the faith of religion and the truths of philosophy are put together under the regime of sadhana, then the secret of true Religion makes itself known. But without sadhana the entire experiment goes the way of inevitable failure. As the great Swami stated, simply and directly, *"My children, the secret of religion lies not in theories, but in practice."* India struck upon the pivotal axioms of philosophy long before other countries, and this feat was accomplished mainly by acknowledging the role of sadhana in life.

The test of the secret of sadhana leading to dharmic Religion lies in its being incomparable among all the purificatory systems and methods of the world, right on up to and inclusive of modern man's experiments with medicine, metaphysics, and psychology. The ceaseless rounds of physical, mental, intellectual, and spiritual suffering that still haunt and harry mankind in contemporary times should have proved to us by now that our physical exercises, food fads, invasive surgeries, ongoing therapy sessions, and parlor room séances are not going to rid life and mind of what ails us. A much more practical approach, say, of accepting Lord Buddha's dictum of the *"suffering-laden nature of human existence*" might be the wiser pathway upon which to proceed — if proceed we would. Then, putting all inferior methods away, or at least just leaving them in the arenas where they apply, the loftier and more crucial business of purity of character, peace of mind, acquisition of wisdom, development of compassion, attainment of enlightenment, and engaging in the service of God in mankind, could be addressed and gracefully executed. And sadhana — not the above and aforementioned substitutes — would be on hand to ensure success rather than mimic it.

The Age-old Dilemma of Monk and Householder

Much like in business and politics, the same shifting of power and perspective has been going on for ages in the realm of religion and spiritual life. In this arena, the brunt of attention is always moving from the monastic vocation to that of the householder, with each body taking its turn at the reins of leadership and guidance over phases of time. Regarding this press, Sri Ramakrishna has said: *"The householder's light is rather like that of a lamp inside of a house, while the sannyasin's light is like that of the sun."* Still, and since all light is subject to darkness in this world, monastic institutions and the priestclass have allowed the ideal to fall many a time. Vivekananda noted this scathingly, even in India: *"Monks and sannyasins and brahmins of a certain type have thrown the country into ruin. Intent all the while on theft and wickedness, these pose as teachers of religion! They will take gifts from the people and at the same time cry, 'Don't touch me!' And what great things they have been doing. 'If a potato happens to touch a brinjal, how long will the universe last before it is deluged?' Or, 'If they do not apply earth a dozen times to clean their hands, will fourteen generations of ancestors go to hell, or twenty-four?' For intricate problems like these they have been finding scientific explanations for the last two-thousand years, while one fourth of the people are starving."*

But the Swami also came to the West and saw what countries and societies of householders had done with religion. Observing over time, he concluded that, though apparently in a fine and fettle condition outwardly, in all actuality it was not a pretty picture — even set against the unfortunate predicament of his own country: *"There is but one basis of well-being, social, political or spiritual; to know that I and my brother are one. This is true for all countries and all people. And Westerners, let me say, will realize it more quickly than Orientals, who have almost exhausted themselves in formulating the idea and producing a few cases of individual realization. Yet it is the tendency to bring everything down to the level of a machine that has given the West its wonderful prosperity. And it is this which has driven away all religion from its doors. Even the little that is left, the West has reduced to a systematic drill. In religion they practice either hypocrisy or fanaticism."*

To avoid both of these extremes — the greed and hypocrisy of the priest class and the sterility of a secularly-based conventional religion — the householder will need to embrace the dharma, taking its vows and precepts seriously and implementing them into daily life in the world. For, from practice of dharma comes revelation of *svadharma*, one's highest direction, which itself leads to all that has purely to do with enlightenment. As Swami Vivekananda has said in this regard: *"Doctrines have been expounded enough. There are books by the millions. Oh, for an ounce of practice!"*

What Sadhana Looks Like in Daily Life

The daily life of a dharmic family would look like this: rising early in the morning for worship followed by recitation and memorization of the scriptures, the essential element of communion with the *Ishtam* (Chosen Ideal) and meditation on Formless Reality (Brahman/God/Allah, etc.) would next ensue. The work of the day could then be taken up, but not without an emphasis on performing it as worship according to the laws of *Karma Yoga*. Once a day, as well, teachings from the guru would be imbibed or, failing that due to lack of easy proximity, the parents would instruct the children in wisdom teachings designed to remove ignorance and instill balance of mind. In the evening there would be worship around the altar, and meditation before sleep in order to neutralize all the residue that may have accumulated in the mind during the day in the field of action.

This combination of inner practice and outer work ensures equanimity of mind amidst the trials and tribulations of the world, and is thus the proverbial grinding stone upon which the impediments and limitations of mind, intellect, and ego get worn away. Even the diseases of the body, inevitable in their appearance, will get gradually and systematically reduced, all the while acting as lessons upon which to learn and actually incorporate the art of balance of mind. What is more, the combination of *jnanam* and *dhyanam* — wisdom and meditation — will "open up avenues" to spiritual experience and realization wherein fresh insight will visit the mind in a flood that will dilute and wash away all traces of ignorance from the mind, and fear and doubt along with it. Lubricated by the warm oil of devotion for God, Truth, Freedom, and all other mainstays of spiritual life, the human body/mind mechanism will become a fit instrument through which to reach the Goal of human existence, serving God in all beings in the interim.

Principles, Not Personalities

If we are to look earnestly at the conditions prevalent in the world during any given span of time, and with any prevailing group of individuals, it becomes evident that it is most efficacious to study those phases of time and especial groups of beings under whose watchful gaze and guiding hand religion flourished for a time. India is ripe for such scrutiny, as it has concerned itself with matters of the Spirit for millennia. While in the body, and with his bird's-eye view of the contemporary goings-on of the world in both of its spheres, Eastern and Western, Swami Vivekananda could see where the real fabric of religion and philosophy was hiding. And despite his appreciation for the West's positive attributes and strong points, his long-time fealty for the Eternal Religion of the ancient Rishis — *Sanatana Dharma* — went undiminished. Acting as a prime example for those of his country who were to come after him, the great Swami envisioned a way in which the best elements of East and West could be fused — but using spirituality, not materialism, for the basis. Writing to a devotee in a letter, he stated: *"There is only one country in the world that understands religion — it is India; that with all their faults the Hindus are head and shoulders above all other nations in morality and spirituality. And that with the proper care and attempt and struggle of all her disinterested sons, by combining some of the active and heroic elements of the West with the calm virtues of the Hindus, there will come a type of men far superior to any that have ever been in this world."*

There is no doubt that the prime workers who manned the fields of early transformation of mind in recent times, and whose guidance in setting up the parameters based upon eternal principles via which spiritually benighted mankind would gain access to "That" which is beyond materialistic science and conventional religion, were monks. For, it requires that if a man would be spiritual, and would move to express that spirituality in the world of human beings, that he must renounce all other undertakings and focus upon, as the *Upanisads* record it, *"That one Thing by which knowing all else is known."*

This well may be the case with regards to authentic spirituality, but such movements and their principles, though incepted in the minds of saints, sages, and seers, were always manifested and put to the test by the thousands of laymen, or householders, who heard the call of Truth and rallied to Its cause. For, even celibate monks will need a physical platform, like the human body, in which to enact and guide both men and movements towards the Light of Reality, and it is the householder who can and should provide that platform.

The problem here is whether the realized soul looking for parents in an age of darkness can find ones who are both worthy of such a boon and able to raise a spiritual child. This would require, among other things, some deep inner abilities such as recognizing the soul's unique stature combined with watchful wariness so as to refrain from routing the young charge towards the superficial things of the world, and worldly life. Here, we are to pause and take a look at our own country in present times, and see how few illumined souls, if any, have incarnated here — the obvious reason being the lack of spiritual knowledge and higher Awareness in potential parents of the West.

And it is here where the problems of a lack of a spiritual education become most pronounced. The timeless principles of the Indian scriptures, both qualified and nondual, are not known in present day times and climes by the rest of the world. The people of these modern times do not know that the Soul of mankind is birthless and deathless; they have not seen or even conceived of the incomparable vision of God with form and beyond form; they have not experienced the bliss of inner communion with Divine Reality via meditation and its outcome, namely *samadhi* or *nirvana*. Most likely, many of them have never even heard of the glories of the Spirit, what to speak of considering them to be real — and far short of conceiving them as an ultimate Goal for life. Were you an illumined soul in search of a conscious embodiment (humorously called a "womb with a view" in spiritual circles) among beings who could first, give you the dharmic teachings and, second, keep you free of maya's clutches, would you take birth in such a country? More likely, certain householders in India or Tibet might feel the impending force of your next visit to *namarupa* — the realm of name and form.

Householders of the Dharma

In spiritual life, like most other areas of occupation, preparation is all the need. And the crucial type of readiness that prepares one for great ideas and great souls is facilitated by sadhana. It must be brought back, or introduced, as the case may be, into the Western household, into all homes and societies, if the ills of this world and the grave mistakes of our forefathers are to be rectified. In short, karma is to be taken to task and neutralized, and this, again, requires sadhana. It would have been better if karma had never accrued in the first place. But since this is not the case here, and beings of this day and time do not know how to live a life free of karmic repercussion and psychic residue, then they must begin to allow the force of spiritual self-effort and the heat of austerity to do their work. Then, in due time, and with this special type of preparation in stages, there will come to the West and among its householders some special souls who are capable of internal transformation and realization, rather than the shallow and immature run of the mill souls which have been incarnating in hoards, in ignorance, for so long. With increased wisdom becoming the property of the masses, we would also see the demise of the charlatan, the opportunist, the religious entrepreneur, and the greedy merchant of the spiritual marketplace. As Swami Vivekananda so aptly puts it: *"The real spiritual man is broad everywhere. His love forces him to be so. Those to whom religion is a trade, are forced to become narrow and mischievous by their introduction into religion of the competitive, fighting and selfish methods of the world. I pity them. It is not their fault. They are children, yay, veritable children, though they be great and high in society. Their eyes see nothing beyond their little horizon of a few yards — the routine of work, eating, drinking, earning, and begetting, following each other in mathematical precision. They know nothing beyond happy little souls! Their sleep is never disturbed. Their nice little brown studies of lives never rudely shocked by the wail of woe, of misery, of degradation and poverty, that has filled the Indian atmosphere — the result of centuries of oppression. They little dream of the ages of tyranny, mental, moral, and physical, that has reduced the image of God to a mere beast of burden; the emblem of the Divine Mother to a slave to bear children; and life itself a curse."*

A More Holy Matrimony of Dharma and Artha

A final word can be said about sadhana, and it applies not only to religion in the world, but also to the application of dharma within the household. Mixing relations in the world with spiritual life and practice, though it may seem inevitable, even beneficial, is guarded against by the knowers and lovers of God. The practitioner should emulate this stance. As the sages of other eastern countries expressed it, one cannot mix God and Mammon. The two can and will exist side by side, but each must have its own specific realm of operation — at least up and until the realized soul can move about in the world as if it were nothing other than Divine Reality in manifested form. This is a tall order, on the level of seeing God in everything. Even action, here, is not itself, transforming into spontaneous consciousness.

Like oil and water, then, which seem to mix at first, then separate completely from one another within seconds, the practice of spirituality must be kept pure, immiscible, free of the insinuations of the world. The same would hold true for the world of business, politics, finance (*artha*), and the dealings of society. As the great Swami so clearly put it: *"We agree with those who say, 'What has religion to do with social reforms?' But they must also agree with us when we tell them that religion has no business to formulate social laws and insist on the difference between beings, because its aim and end obliterate all such fictions and monstrosities. If it be pleaded that through this difference we would reach final equality and unity, we answer that this same religion has said over and over again that mud cannot be washed by mud. As if a man can be moral by being immoral! Social laws were created by economic conditions under the sanction of religion. The terrible mistake of religion was to interfere in social matters."*

To avoid the obfuscating overlays of the five senses in nature, the distortions of the human mind in maya, or even to learn from the mistakes of the past and adjust ourselves and our cultures properly, the spiritual ideal must be held sacrosanct, its incomparable standard never compromised. To try this ideal of spiritual practice in daily life in its own setting, and according to its own rules and requirements, would be to hold up its precious tenets in contrast against the many centuries of attempts and failures that secular life and conventional religion have shown us. In effect, what would get revealed is the vast difference, both in quality and in efficacy, between what Indian seers termed the *Jnana Marga* and the *Bhoga Marga* — The path of wisdom and the path of pleasure.

Following in the way of the latter, called the "path of pleasure," family life in the home not only loses its luster and its meaning, but gradually contributes to an overall loss of closeness and camaraderie and the feelings of unrest and enmity that ensue. By following the way of the path of wisdom, however, the family, the society, even the entire nation, might enter into a golden age where spiritual practice is not only duly and willingly engaged in, but venerated by all for its ability to destroy the poisons of relative existence, exalt mankind to the noble status of divinity, and vault the aspiring soul into the vast reaches of insight and realization that best represent his own innate and ever-pure divine nature.

Babaji Bob Kindler is the Spiritual Director of the SRV Associations with centers in Hawaii, Oregon, and California. A teacher of religion and spirituality and a prolific author, his books include *The Avadhut, Twenty-Four Aspects of Mother Kali, Ten Divine Articles of Sri Durga, Sri Sarada Vijnanagita, Swami Vivekananda Vijnanagita, An Extensive Anthology of Sri Ramakrishna's Stories, A Quintessential Yoga Vasishtha, Reclaiming Kundalini Yoga, and others*. Founder and Artistic Director of Jai Ma Music, he is also an accomplished musician and composer who has produced over twenty-five albums of instrumental and devotional music to date.

Preliminary Practices to Mantra and Meditation

A Householder's Nine-fold Ritual Prior to Daily Spiritual Practice

- **Nityasarga** – Wakening consciously each day

- **Sandhya** – Purificatory bath and rituals

- **Pranams** – Prostrations at the altar

- **Dirgha Pranava** – Long recitation of "Om"

- **Prapatti** – Prayer for fulfillment

- **Samarpana** – Offering one's life to God

- **Purusha Yajna** – Dedicating the soul to God

- **Guru-pranam** – Salutations to one's Gurus

- **Utsaha-vrata** – Vow to infuse sadhana with enthusiasm

"Nonrecitation of the scriptures is the rust of monasteries, nonexertion in spiritual practice is the rust of households; sloth is the rust of all that is truly beautiful; negligence is the rust of the spiritual vigil."

– Lord Buddha in the Dhammapada

◆ *Rabbi Rami Shapiro*

≈ MENSCHCRAFT ≈
WHAT WOULD A MENSCH DO?
An Introduction to Living Wisely & Well

For the general solution for many of the basic ills of this world, Swami Vivekananda has uttered the words, *"Be good, do good. This is the essence of all religion."* This simple advice far outstrips any of the fine philosophy that spiritually awakened, sensitive living beings can engage in — at least so far as bringing overall peace and balance back to this troubled world at this present time is concerned.

What is a Mensch? Mensch is a Yiddish word for a person who thinks and acts in ways that make the world a little more just, good, and compassionate. Everyone has the ability to be a mensch.

Menschen (the plural of mensch) aren't born; they are made — self-made as a matter of fact. No matter how you grew up, no matter in what circumstances you presently find yourself, you are capable of being a mensch — of acting for the good, the just, and the compassionate. It may not be easy, but it is never impossible. It is a matter of will.

It is popular today to say that people are inherently good, and that society or circumstance makes them evil. This is contrary to menschtalk. People are born with the capacity for both good and evil, but nobody is born inherently good or evil. Being a mensch is doing good even when capable of doing evil.

Denying your capacity for evil leaves you open to blindly doing evil. Unless you are personally aware of your capacity for evil and take responsibility for it, you will excuse the evil you do and rationalize your behavior. Only when you know you are capable of both good and evil, can you honestly judge your actions and direct yourself into life enhancing and menschlich (mensch-like) behaviors. Accepting your capacity for evil and your capacity for good is the fundamental prerequisite for mastering the skills of Menschcraft.

Where is Your Mensch?

Lots of people believe that deep inside of you lives the perfect you, and that all you have to do to become the person you where meant to be is to turn inward and find that perfect you. There are two problems with this kind of thinking. First, the notion of perfection as a static state attainable once and for all. Second, the notion that the real work is inner work, thus disengaging you from the world around you.

Menschcraft offers an alternative to this view. You are already the "you" you were meant to be. Yet you are not a static being, fixed and unchanging. On the contrary, you are forever changing and perfectible. Instead of thinking of yourself as a "human being," think of yourself as a "human becoming." Thinking in terms of becoming allows you to think in terms of process. You are a process unfolding in time and space, and as a process you are never perfect and always perfectible. Perfection is not a goal you can attain, but an on-going process of making today a little more just and compassionate than yesterday; and tomorrow a little more just and compassionate than today. You don't have to be someone else to be better than you are at this moment. There is no real you, no true self that is buried inside. There is only the "you" you are at this very moment.

Escape or Engage?

Menschcraft is not about escaping from your present self to find your true self. Menschcraft is about engaging the self you are and moving forward. Escaping from yourself in order to find yourself is a ruse that keeps you from paying attention to what is going on around and within you. Paying attention is the key to moving forward. Paying attention allows you to see what is happening as if you were an actor on a stage. Viewing your life as if you were an actor allows you to be part of the play and removed from the play at the same time.

Being part of the play, you are called upon to give each moment, each encounter, your full attention and energy. You engage each scene fully and without hesitation.

Being removed from the play allows you to step back and observe what it is you are doing. From this vantage point you see how your own behavior produces good and evil. You see how your own mind helps invent conflict by separating you from others and narrowing your focus to "I," "me," and "mine."

Seeing how your mind generates conflict, you find yourself able to observe the conflict without investing yourself and your emotional energy in the conflict. The conflict still exists, but you are able to see how both sides contribute to furthering the conflict. Seeing this free from emotional attachment allows you to see a way through the conflict that affirms both yourself and the other.

The more you learn to observe your encounters the more you realize that you are never separate from the people, things or events you encounter. Both you and they are part of a larger play. Free from the notion of separation — you against them — your whole sense of life changes and you find yourself feeling lighter, less controlled by, and more in control of what you do.

Ultimately you begin to see the world as an extension of

> "Menschcraft is not about escaping from your present self to find your true self. Menschcraft is about engaging the self you are and moving forward. Escaping from yourself in order to find yourself is a ruse that keeps you from paying attention to what is going on around and within you. Paying attention is the key to moving forward."

yourself and yourself as an extension of the world; and both as extensions of Life. You see that everything goes with everything else; that all is interdependent and co–arising in the never ending round of birth and death. Knowing this you find yourself ever more able to engage Life with justice and compassion. And this ability makes you a mensch.

Why Are You Here?

You were born into this world to bring about a transformation. In menschtalk this transformation is called *tikkun*. Tikkun means healing, repairing, transforming.

Think of the world as an immense jigsaw puzzle whose pieces are scattered everywhere and whose inherent meaning is jumbled and incoherent. The pieces need to be reconnected so that the picture, the world's inherent meaning and coherence, becomes clear. You are the means by which the pieces are repaired to the whole.

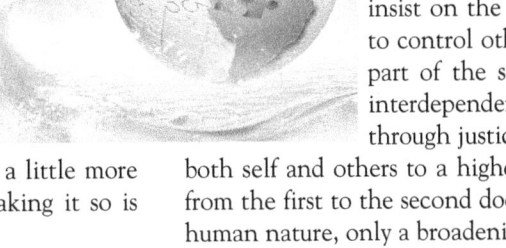

The pieces of the world puzzle are the events, people, things, problems, concerns and conflicts you encounter every day. Handled with grace, humor, justice and compassion, each of these is lifted up and reconnected to the whole. One act at a time, the world becomes a little more peaceful, loving, just and compassionate. And making it so is what being a mensch is all about.

The world, like people, is neither inherently good nor inherently evil. The world, like people, is inherently perfectible. Not that the world or people will ever attain perfection, but that both people and the world can become a little better today compared to what each was yesterday. A mensch is never stuck in yesterday. A mensch is never content to blame habit, family or society for the problems of self. A mensch isn't much interested in blame. A mensch simply acknowledges what is and seeks to bring about what might be by acting rightly, even if for the first time. After all, this is why you were born.

A Middle Way

Menschcraft is not about erasing yourself in service to others, but discovering that self and other are partners in the process of tikkun, perfecting the world. Menschcraft is a celebration and an uplifting of both self and other, and by other we mean not only people, but things as well. The mensch has respect for all Life, animate and inanimate, human and otherwise. Menschcraft does not value the self more or less than the other, but sees the two as part of a greater whole. This is an important distinction that makes Menschcraft a middle way between the more popular extremes of egoism and asceticism.

Egoism says that the self is all that matters. Whatever you do you do for yourself. There is no act that is not selfish; no kindness that is not self-serving. You do what you do in order to get what you want. If getting what you want requires you to treat others with respect, then you will treat them with respect. If getting what you want does not require respect, then respect is of no interest to you. Right and wrong are determined solely by the desires of the self. Asceticism is the opposite of egoism. Asceticism says that the self is the source of all evil. If you would save the world, end the self. Ending the self requires you to deny the self its every desire. Eventually the self desires nothing. A desireless self is no longer a self, and thus the evil is eliminated.

Menschcraft takes the middle ground, seeing the self as both part of the problem and part of the solution: part of the problem when you insist on the illusion of separateness and seek to control others in order to attain your ends; part of the solution when you recognize the interdependence of self and others, and seek through justice, compassion, and respect to lift both self and others to a higher level of engagement. To move from the first to the second does not require a radical change in human nature, only a broadening of your awareness of the situation in which you find yourself. This is a key part of Menschcraft.

Start Where You Are

Menschcraft starts with you as you are: imperfect and perfectible. A wonderfully insightful Hasidic saying puts it this way: "No matter how hard you try or which way you stir its contents, a pot of garbage is still a pot of garbage. Better to leave the pot alone and spend your time doing something constructive."

A mensch isn't perfect, only perfectible. A mensch makes mistakes, but rarely the same one twice. A mensch has her pot of garbage, yet puts her energies in doing good in the present rather than stirring up the past. Dwelling on past error is never as valuable as doing good in the present. When you do something wrong admit it, apologize, and work to set it right; learn from the mistakes you make so as not to repeat them; and then move on. Dwelling on errors and fretting over your natural inclination to selfishness is just self-centered whining. Beginning with yourself doesn't mean excusing mistakes or raising them to the level of absolute preoccupation. Both extremes are escapes from the real challenge of living.

Principles of Menschcraft

Menschcraft is the art of being a mensch. It isn't about being perfect but about perfecting being. It isn't about escaping from the realities of this world but about engaging them fully, attentively, with justice and compassion. Some 2000 years ago the great and great-hearted Rabbi Hillel articulated the Three Principles of Menschcraft: 1) If I am not for myself, who will be for me? 2) If I am only for myself, what am I? and 3) If not now, when? Understanding and applying these three principles to your life is the practice of Menschcraft.

from the world, but a part of it. To be for yourself requires you to be for the world; to be for the world requires you to be for yourself. The two are, at root, one.

A mensch sees and lives this oneness. A mensch sees all things as interconnected, and knows that to be for yourself you have to be for others as well. There is no alternative.

This is not a matter of choosing between being for yourself or being for others, it is a matter of recognizing that to be for yourself requires you to be for others, and to be for others requires you to be for yourself.

> "You are not apart from the world, but a part of it. To be for yourself requires you to be for the world; to be for the world requires you to be for yourself. The two are, at root, one. A mensch sees and lives this oneness. A mensch sees all things as interconnected, and knows that to be for yourself you have to be for others as well. There is no alternative."

If I Am not for Myself, Who Will Be For Me?

Being for yourself means being honest with and about your shortcomings without allowing concern with them to keep you from doing good.

If you are not for yourself — that is if you are empty of self-respect; if you are obsessed with the wrongs you have done; if you are incapable of recognizing your gifts and your strengths — who can possibly be for you? If you can't stand yourself no one else can stand you either.

If you are not for yourself, you are against yourself. You are your own worst enemy, and lead the world in a battle against your natural ability to do what it is you can do to make this world a little better for your having been born into it.

If you imagine you are incapable of being any better than you have been in the past you abdicate responsibility for the present and the future. This abdication gives you license to wallow in self-pity, and for many people this is their one great delight. It is the antithesis of Menschcraft.

Being for yourself means taking responsibility for perfecting yourself. No one can do it for you. Yet, once you begin the process of perfectibility you find you never have to do it alone. If you love and respect yourself; if you accept your limitations gracefully and then move beyond them purposefully; if you admit your fears and your errors honestly and then overcome them constructively; if you choose to make the world a little kinder for your being in it; you discover that the world is suddenly allied with you. The whole world seems to conspire for your success. Being for yourself invites and allows others to be for you as well.

If I Am Only for Myself, What Am I?

When you are truly for yourself, you discover a deep and compelling desire to be for others as well, and being for others invites them to be for you. The two principles feed into each other.

The more purposefully you act for tikkun, the uplifting of the world with justice and compassion, the more clearly you understand that you and the world go together. You are not apart

The notion of choosing presupposes a chooser, a separate self weighing real options. The mensch sees this seemingly separate self as an illusion, and acts from a place of awareness far deeper than choice.

Imagine you are holding a sharp sword in your right hand. What are the chances that you would choose to cut off your left hand? Unless cutting off your left hand is necessary to save your life, chances are you wouldn't even entertain the notion. Cutting off your hand is not an option; therefore not cutting off your hand cannot be called a choice.

When you engage life as a mensch you come to see that the world and yourself go together. You and the world are the right and left hands of Life, so to speak. Harming one will harm both.

As a mensch you do what is right because you know what is real. In Hebrew, this doing from knowing is called mitzaveh, being commanded. The command comes not from an external or internal authority, but from the realization of the interconnectedness of self and world. As soon as you realize the unity of self and other you feel overwhelmingly commanded to act for the good of both.

If Not Now, When?

Hillel's Third Principle of Menschcraft, If Not Now, When, is a call to action. If not now, when will you realize your *menschlichkeit*, your capacity to be a mensch, and use it for the betterment of yourself and others? The answer is — never. There is only now: the past and the future are figments of the imagination. Only the now, the present, is happening.

Menschcraft is engaging this very moment with respect, compassion and justice. When you operate out of the past or project into the future, you sift through your memory and piece together a drama that seems to fit a given situation and then respond to that situation as if it were the other.

The advantage of this kind of behavior is that it gives you a clear script to follow. There is less anxiety over not knowing what to say or do because you are saying and doing things you have said and done before. You avoid facing the present by covering it over with habits from the past.

Living from the past is living in the past; and living in the past means you are not grounded in the reality of the present. If you are not grounding yourself, your behavior, and your feelings in the present, then you are not fully engaging Life at all.

The mensch works in and with the present. You are not ignorant of the past; you simply don't let the past overpower the present. You are not disinterested in the future; you simply focus your energy on the present. Ask yourself, "Am I dealing with the reality of this moment, or is this some scenario I've concocted to avoid dealing with the present?" If you ask the question honestly, you will know the true answer.

Core Values of Menschcraft

Hillel's Three Principles are like a compass, they help you stay on course by pointing to the ideal of menschlichkeit. But a compass all by itself isn't a journey, it just points toward one. In addition to a compass you need to take actual steps. These steps are the ways in which you live out the values of a mensch. What are the values of a mensch? There are three, and they come from the Bible where the Prophet Micah tells the people just what it is God requires of them: Do justly, act kindly, and walk humbly with your God. (Micah 6:8) Living Micah's core values is how we live up to the Three Principles of Hillel.

When you do justly, you make sure that your actions not only serve yourself and your personal needs, but that they also do no harm to anyone else. As Hillel said, you must be for yourself, but not only for yourself.

When you act kindly, you put other people first. You make room for other people in your life — making room for their needs, their ideas, their desires. Of course if you only make room for others and never make room for yourself, you are violating Hillel's First Principle. Try to balance the need for self and other, and see if you can't make room for both in your life.

Walking humbly with your God is often hard for people to understand. First of all why humbly? The Torah tells us that what people do matters. Actions have consequences. What you do matters not just to yourself but to everyone else. Your actions are like a rock thrown into a pool of water. While the rock only hits one small part of the pool, the ripples from the rock's impact can affect the entire pool. You may pretend that your actions affect you alone, but you would be wrong. You are the world and you have a responsibility toward its well being. Being humble means that you accept that responsibility and act in a manner that takes the needs of the whole into account.

Why does Micah say "your" God and not just God? Because people have differing ideas about God. Some people don't speak of God at all. What Micah is saying is that you have to respect the many different ideas about God that people have, and not imagine that any one idea is the one true idea. Being humble means knowing that your idea about God is just that — an idea. And God is greater than any idea we can imagine.

But what if you don't believe in God at all? Can you still be a mensch? Of course. Being a mensch is about cultivating justice, kindness, and humility in yourself and the world. If your idea of God helps you do this, fine. If you feel no need of God in your quest for justice, kindness, and humility, also fine. What counts is what you do, not what you believe.

And yet, God is important. Judaism has spoken of and relied upon God for over 3000 years. God is central to everything Jewish, even being a mensch. And while you can act justly, kindly, and humbly without having any idea about or interest in God, still a mensch cannot ignore God.

So what is God? Jews have debated this question forever, and have come up with the following conclusion: Nobody knows and nobody can know. All we know is that there is something greater than us. Call it nature, call it The Force, call it God, call it Tao, there is something that unites all life into a single system; something that manifests laws of nature as well as laws of the spirit. Just as there are laws that govern the workings of physical things, so there are laws that govern the workings of spiritual things.

What are the spiritual laws? You know them already; they are written on your heart that you can do them. (Jeremiah 31:33) They are being just, kind, and humble. They are respecting self and other. They are the values and principles of menschlichkeit.

When you act like a mensch the world grows a little saner, a little more gentle, a little more loving. When you act against the laws of the spirit, when you seek only to serve yourself and not others, when you don't care about justice and kindness, but only about yourself and your needs and desires, the world becomes more harsh, a little more violent, and more frightening.

You cannot decide for yourself to violate the law of gravity, but you can decide to violate the principles of values of menschlichkeit. If you could not do so, there would be no need to ask: What Would a Mensch Do? The question makes sense, because you are free to act anyway you wish— like a mensch or not like a mensch. It is always up to you. Asking What Would a Mensch Do reminds you of your ability to affect the world for good or ill. Answering What Would a Mensch Do with justice, kindness, and humility, means you are a mensch and the world can smile just a bit more.

Rabbi Rami Shapiro is an award-winning author, poet, essayist, and educator whose poems have been anthologized in over a dozen volumes, and whose prayers are used in prayer books around the world. Rami received rabbinical ordination from the Hebrew Union College–Jewish Institute of Religion and holds doctoral degrees in both Jewish studies and divinity. A congregational rabbi for 20 years, Rabbi Shapiro currently teaches Religious Studies at Middle Tennessee State University, and directs One River (**www.one-river.org**), a not-for-profit educational foundation devoted to building community through contemplative conversation. Rami writes a regular column for Spirituality and Health Magazine called Roadside Assistance on Your Spiritual Journey. His most recent books are The Sacred Art of Lovingkindness, The Divine Feminine, and Open Secrets from which this essay was adapted. Rabbi Rami can be reached through his website, **www.rabbirami.com**

Svadhyaya (continued from page 23)

Svadhyaya facilitates this to a tremendous degree by imbedding the dharma in the mind, not just in the brain. I once heard the following story about a man in India. He was quite elderly, but every day he would go to the library and study *Sanskrit*, the sacred, revelatory language of India. He did not begin his Sanskrit studies until his life was nearly over. Someone asked him one day, "Sir, why are you studying Sanskrit now? Isn't it a little late? You can't possibly master it now." But the man replied, "True, but I am studying for my next lifetime." Thus, if one has samskaras for spiritual life, the early practice of svadhyaya will open up the inner memory of one's knowledge gained in prior lifetimes. And if one does not have such samskaras, svadhyaya is an efficient method for creating them. Dharmic parents will pay attention to this and start their children early in the memorization of beautiful, noble verses. It can be a joyful, divine pastime together.

This discussion of samskaras, meditation, and Swami Vivekananda's statement about knowledge being inherent in the mind, leads next to one of the most esoteric benefits of svadhyaya. It requires a brief introduction. We do not have only an individual mind. At the individual level most beings are only conscious of that part of the mind connected to the brain, which dies eventually. However, the brain is transcended daily but unconsciously in the states of dream and dreamless sleep, and can be transcended consciously in deep meditation and samadhi – this is the position of Yoga Psychology and the direct experience of the seers and yogis. The so-called individual mind is part of a vast collective and cosmic mind consisting of the minds of those beings in every realm of existence: humans, ancestors, angels, celestials, and deities, all the way to *Brahma, Vishnu*, and *Siva*, the Trinity responsible for projecting, sustaining, and eventually dissolving all realms of existence at the time of *pralaya*.

When an adept yogi or yogini enters deep meditation or samadhi, or consciously enters the states of dream and deep sleep, she finds this collective and cosmic mind within her own Self. Having seen this in a deeply aware state, this knowledge remains accessible upon returning to the "normal" state of mind in the waking state. One of the technical ways of describing this is that the yogis have opened up *nadis*, which are like nerves in our subtle body/mind through which consciousness travels between states of awareness such as: dreaming and dreamless sleep, ascension up the chakras, and to the different heavenly realms described by many religious systems. The difference between the adept yogis and everyone else is the remembrance resulting from opening up these nadis. Further, those who have achieved this no longer take the body (physical or subtle) to be the Self and are able to exit the body at death consciously and fearlessly. This, in turn, facilitates a conscious rebirth for those who return to embodiment for further purification or to help awaken others. Spiritual practices like svadhyaya, meditation, and profound worship are all ways of opening up these nadis, and when they open, we not only have access to all knowledge, but regain memory of our eternal existence, ever free of modifications like body, senses, mind, and ego.

When we memorize scripture, it may seem that we are adding knowledge into the mind. Rather, we are breaking down resistance blocking one's entry into the inner realms (i.e., opening the nadis), formed by lifetimes of preoccupation with physical experiences in the waking state, which unguided by dharma, lead to endless karmic distractions. Not only do these pose formidable obstacles to spiritual practice, they oppose revelation that one's mind is a gateway into the collective mind of beings and the cosmic mind of God wherein all knowledge exists. By practicing svadhyaya we are using higher knowledge as an intellectual chisel to get at the source of all knowledge and realization within our Self.

How do we begin? First, it is important to set the atmosphere. This is a formal part of one's *sadhana*, spiritual practice. Study and memorization should be practiced in a place set aside for this purpose in one's home, which is free from distractions. A shrine or meditation room is excellent. Alternatively, a natural setting, such as the mountains, desert, forest, or beach, away from people is also good since these are conducive to deep reflection. Sit with back comfortably straight as for meditation. Before beginning, pray inwardly for wisdom, devotion, sincerity, and humility. Svadhyaya is best practiced as part of kriya yoga: austerity, study/recitation, and self-surrender. It is recommended to learn one or more of the Vedic Peace chants and recite one before each session. Learning all seven peace chants in Sanskrit and English is how members of the SRV Associations sangha are launched into svadhyaya as a practice. After learning those, we memorize seven meditation chants, seven wisdom chants, and seven universal chants, all drawn from the *Upanisads, Bhagavad Gita, Vivekachudamani,* and other scriptures.

Leave time daily to practice and contemplate verses already learned and to learn another. This practice is ideal for householders who do not have the time to study many scriptures. Memorization and deep contemplation of one verse each day or week is more fruitful and profound than reading through a variety of scriptures to "check them off one's list." One must also guard against mindless recitation resulting from rushing to complete one's daily practice, as well as from frequent repetition and the presence of tamas in the mind, dulling one's sensitivity to inspiration. Truth does not change, only the mind. Thus, the vow of *utsaha*, fresh enthusiasm for the dharma, is cherished and cultivated by all sincere practitioners.

In conclusion, svadhyaya is an indispensable practice for engendering balance in earthly life, creation of essential samskaras for the spiritual journey, and access to the infinite storehouse of wisdom existing within us.

Annapurna Sarada is the president of SRV Associations and an assistant teacher for the sangha and its children. She also writes a blog for Advaita-Academy.org. To read more about SRV's children's classes and retreats, visit the newsletter archive on SRV's website: www.srv.org

The Three Dispositions of Living Beings

"The faith of embodied beings is on accordance with their natural disposition. Beings are of the nature of their faith; what their faith is, that verily they are."
— Sri Krishna

Chart by Babaji Bob Kindler   Property of SRV Associations

	Worship	Food	Sacrifices	Austerities	Gifts
Sattvika Being	The Devas (Good/Noble)	Pure, Savory, Substantial	Motivelessness	3-Fold Austerity (**)	Selfless & timely
Rajasika Being	Yakshas & Rakshasas (Proud/Warlike)	Sour, Saline, Pungent	Expectation of Reward	For Gain & Fame	Expectation with Grudge
Tamasika Being	Pretas/Bhutas (Dull/Fearful)	Stale, Impure, & Overcooked	Contrary to Ordinances	Self-torture & Destruction	Heedless & Insulting

** The Threefold Austerity of Sattvik Beings

Austerity of the Body	Austerity of Speech	Austerity of Mind
Worshiping the Gods	Truthful Speech	Silence of Thought
Reverence for the Wise	Beneficial Speech	Gentleness
Purity of Act	Inspiring Speech	Mental Control
Uprightness	Calming Speech	Fresh Disposition
Noninjury	Sacred Recitation	Selflessness

The Three Karmic Accruals of Living Beings

	Characteristic	Quality	Effect	Path
Sattva	Luminosity	Happiness	Knowledge	Pure Worlds
Rajas	Passion	Activity	Selfish Desire	Labor
Tamas	Ignorance	Delusion	Heedlessness	Suffering

"That one who, formerly was dull and heedless, but after due consideration becomes mindful and vigilant, illumines the world like a moon set free from a cloud." — Lord Buddha

◆ Father Bruno Barnhart

A Return to CHRISTIAN ADVAITA

It has been said that nonduality is at the core of the three great Asian traditions of Hinduism, Buddhism and Taoism. This seems, at first sight, in stark contrast with the Judaeo-Christian tradition. Further reflection and meditation brings one to a different judgment, at least with regard to Christianity. Nonduality is at the heart of the Christian revelation, or Christ-mystery, but one would probably never guess this if acquainted only with the theology and the biblical interpretation of the last few centuries. Western Christianity has evolved very far from the sapiential or wisdom vision of the first twelve centuries. This wisdom Christianity was essentially participative and ultimately unitive.

One can identify Christian Advaita in the New Testament, particularly in the writings attributed to Paul and to John:

"For as many of you as were baptized into Christ have put on Christ. There is neither Jew nor Greek, there is neither slave nor free, there is neither male nor female; for you are all one in Christ Jesus."
(Galatians 3:27-28)

"I and the Father are one."
(John 10:30)

This Christian Advaita is not identical with the Advaita of the Vedanta or with the nondual realization of Zen Buddhism. I believe that it corresponds to these Asian realizations, but with distinct modalities that characterize the Christ-event.

Two difficulties confront us from the outset, in seeking to identify a Christian Advaita. First, there is this distinctiveness and apparent complexity of the Christian experience, which easily obscures its essentially nondual character. The experience seems less pure, less simple, perhaps less completely interior to the individual person.

The second difficulty is related to the centrality of the Word of God in the Judaeo-Christian tradition. To speak of the Word of God in this way has implications which transform the whole picture, the energy of the totality. One is immediately aware of this but usually at a level just beneath clear consciousness when moving between a Hindu or Buddhist world and a Christian world. The Word of God, in the biblical sense, is hyperpersonal: it is a fullness of presence and of power, manifest and active in this world, challenging the human being to a response of the heart and of the whole of one being and life. This Word is understood by Christians to have become a human person in Jesus Christ.

The divine Word, and the Event of its progressive embodiment in human life and history which is centered in the life, death and resurrection of Jesus becomes so central and dominant in Christian tradition that it eclipses every alternative perspective. The absolute authority of the divine Word infuses the doctrines, the laws, the institutional forms of Christianity so pervasively that other dimensions of human life and even of the Mystery itself are suppressed. Only gradually do the different dimensions of human experience begin to manifest themselves in their autonomy. Even when they did appear during the first thousand years of Christianity, they could hardly find expression in other than biblical language, that is, in the symbolic forms which were believed to belong to the divine Word. Nonduality, in particular, could hardly be expressed clearly and directly during these past two millennia. The exceptions have been most often among the mystics. Even there, however, the experience would nearly always be clothed within the symbolic vocabulary of the Christian theological tradition rather than finding a more direct and pure expression in metaphysical or phenomenological language.

Nonduality in the Christian tradition of the first five centuries was expressed, in fact, chiefly in terms of the divine Word itself, in a conception which integrated the Greek philosophical tradition. This was the Logos-theology of the Church fathers, based upon the Prologue of John's Gospel:

*"In the beginning was the Word....
and the Word was made flesh and dwelt among us."*

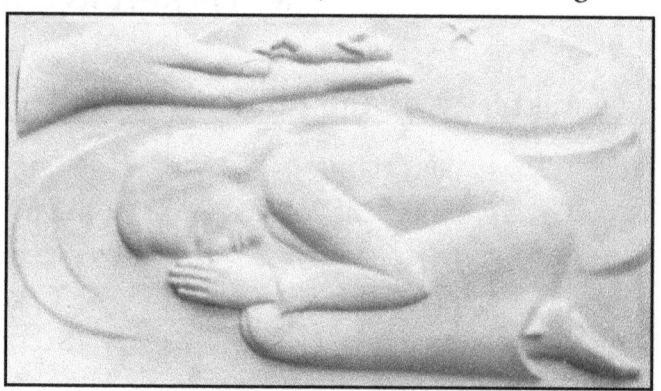

The Difference: Divine Projection.

While nonduality or Advaita may be found in Christianity as well as in the Asian traditions, it is found there with a characteristic dynamic. As I try to express this peculiar thrust of the Christian Deity, however, it will be difficult to find words which do not seem to apply also to the traditions of India. The divine Absolute, in the Christian perspective, is the One; yet this One is internally generative, articulating itself in Word and Spirit, or Mind and Energy. Further, the One overflows outside the Divinity itself, bringing the cosmos, living beings and humanity into existence. Meister Eckhart's expression is evocative: ebullitio, or boiling. The One without beginning seethes within itself in a pure intensity of being, a dance of consciousness and love, Satcidananda. Then in a free outpouring of love, it brings forth the creation.

Speaking lightly, one might say that Christianity knows its God (or Father or One) as extroverted as well as introverted.

Indeed this is a projective, an active One which is continually coming forth from itself in creating other beings, and then coming forth once again to dwell unitively within the beings that it has brought forth. The product of this incessant coming-forth of the One is a dynamic of newness which transforms not only the life of the individual person but history itself. Human life and human history take on a creative dynamism; humanity assumes a role in the evolution of the universe.

Nonduality and the Rebirth of Wisdom Christianity

The Western world, under the mostly subterranean influence of the Christ-event, has been propelled outward and forward into multiplicity. The culture of the modern West is consequently permeated with a radically dualistic mentality. Knowledge, to be valid, must always be objective: that is, knowledge of an other, of an object. Knowledge is always of the parts and their interaction, never of the totality. The revolution which begins to be evident in the new science of a Fritjof Capra, a Rupert Sheldrake or a David Bohm, marks the end of the West's great sapiential parenthesis, the centuries-long period of non-participative consciousness. We begin to perceive the signs of the rebirth of a wisdom tradition in the West, and this also within Christianity. A rebirth of the Christian tradition of wisdom today will be centered, I believe, not only in 1) the divine Word (as before), but in 2) nonduality, or Advaita, and 3) in the emergent person. Advaita rejoins us with the Beginning, with Atman-Brahman, the unitive Source, the uncarved Block, the One. On the other hand, persons not only individual, but communal and cosmic, orient us toward the End, which in biblical language is called the new creation.

Flowering and Eclipse of Nonduality in the West

Despite the constraints we have considered, explicit articulations of nonduality have appeared in the West. The most explicit and most developed of these is the thought of Plotinus, summarized by Lex Hixon in a recent issue of Nectar (vol.2, n.3). Plotinus, the Greek philosopher from whom derives what is called Neoplatonism, was probably the thinker of greatest influence upon Christianity from the third through the twelfth centuries. It is striking that in the very thirteenth century in which the center of gravity of Western Christian thought moved from Plato (and Plotinus) to Aristotle — grandfather of our modern scientific mentality — that a new and distinctive expression of nonduality came forth from within Christianity itself. This appears in its most rigorous philosophical form in Thomas Aquinas, soon to be developed in a more explicit and experiential language by Meister Eckhart, and then in its most fluent mystical form by John Ruysbroeck.

Soon after this flowering, Western Christianity was torn asunder by the Protestant Reformation. The churches, both Protestant and Catholic, assumed an armored, warlike posture which was to make a unitive theological perspective impossible for nearly five centuries. The Second Vatican Council (1962-1965) marks the turning point within Roman Catholicism, when Christianity begins to come out from its elevated fortress under the open sky. Western consciousness begins once again to become aware of the clear, unbounded light at its core.

The reawakening to nonduality within Christianity today is catalyzed by the new contact with the Asian traditions. Implicit in the taking up of Eastern meditation practices in the West is an incipient experience of nonduality. Thomas Merton is one of a number of Christian monks who pursued the nondual experience, satori or sunyata, in contact with the Buddhist traditions. Among those who explicitly sought and reflected upon the Advaitan experience of Hindu Vedanta there stand out a cluster of three Europeans who emigrated to India: Jules Monchanin, Henri Le Saux (Abhishiktananda) and Bede Griffiths. Raimon Panikkar, a professional theologian, engaged with Advaita on a more rigorously philosophical level.

Toward a Christian Advaita

Jules Monchanin (1895-1957) conceived his task and that of his associates as a fresh understanding of the Christian divine Trinity from the perspective of Hindu Advaita.

Abhishiktananda (1910-1973) undertook a radical personal quest for the Advaitan experience, which he related at once to Jesus's experience at his baptism and the experience of Christian baptism. The fullest development of Christian Advaita according to Abhishiktananda is found in John's Gospel, and particularly in the words with which Jesus identifies himself, "I AM." This is a very profound intuition; it may be that here we have the deepest point of contact between Christianity and Vedanta, between the Christian contemplative experience and the experience of Advaita. Bede Griffiths (1906-1993) turned in a different direction, although still in the world of John's Gospel. The true Christian Advaita for Griffiths is found in the communion of love which exists between Jesus and his Father, then participated by the disciples. This is summed up for him in John 17:21-24.

"...that they may all be one; even as you, Father, are in me, and I in you, that they also may be in us, that the world may believe that you have sent me. The glory which you have given me I have given to them, that they may be one even as we are one, I in them and you in me, that they may become perfectly one, so that the world may know that you have sent me and have loved them even as you have loved me."

Christian nonduality may be understood either from the perspective of identity, therefore, or from that of relationship. When understood as an identity with the divine Absolute which constitutes one's own deepest identity, it resonates very strongly with the Advaita of the Vedanta and of Ramana Maharshi.

Father Bruno Barnhart, 1931-2015, was a monk of New Camaldoli Hermitage, Big Sur, California. He was largely occupied with the Christian sapiential (wisdom) tradition and its rebirth in our time. He is author of *The Good Wine: Reading John from the Center* (Paulist Press, 1993) and *Second Simplicity: The Inner Shape of Christianity* (Paulist, 1999), and editor of *The One Light: Bede Griffiths' Principal Writings* (2001).

◆ *John Dobson*

PHYSICS AND VEDANTA

"If, in time and space, the changeless did not show through, we wouldn't have inertia. If the infinite did not show through, we wouldn't have electricity. And if the undivided did not show through, we would not have gravity and the attraction between opposites. Also, if the duality did not keep up the plurality, we wouldn't have the atomic table. And if the plurality did not keep up the duality, we wouldn't have atoms at all. That's how I see it."

Galileo has stated: "*The constitution of the Universe may be put in first place among all natural things that can be known.*" That, of course, is the task of the physicist, to see if he can figure out the constitution of the Universe. And I went to the University of California in 1934 to study bio-chemistry in the hope of keeping Einstein *alive*, so that he could figure it out. But I now believe that it is impossible to figure it out without the help of the Vedantins.

What we now call the philosophy of Vedanta (and I don't mean the practice, but the philosophy behind the practice of what we call Advaita Vedanta) was apparently invented by some very sharp physicists in India a long time ago, because a great deal of that old physics, including the identity of mass and energy (which, in modern times, went from Swami Vivekananda through Tesla to Mileva Einstein) is built into the Sanskrit language, and the language is very old. And those old physicists discovered some very interesting and important physics which we desperately need now if we're going to figure this thing out.

The Sanskrit word for this Universe is *Jagat*, the changing. But those old physicists perceived that, since change is seen against the changeless, there must be, underlying this changing Universe, an existence not in time and space, and therefore, neither changing, finite nor divided. That they called *Brahman*. The problem then arose, "How, then, do we see change? If what exists is changeless, how do we see a Universe of change?" And they said, "It can only be by mistake." So they studied mistakes. If they hadn't studied mistakes, they might not have seen it.

They pointed out that in order to mistake a rope for a snake, there are three things that one must do. First, one must fail to see that it's a rope. (That they called the veiling power of the mistake, *Avarana Shakti*.) Next, one must jump to the conclusion that it's a snake. (That they called the projecting power of the mistake, *Vikshepa Shakti*.) And finally, one must have seen the length and diameter of the rope in the first place or one never would have mistaken it for the length and diameter of a snake. (That they called the revealing power of the mistake, *Prakasha Shakti*.) And that is what is so very important to our physics. It is because of the revealing power, that the changeless, the infinite, the undivided must show in the physics.

Those old physicists sometimes referred to these three aspects of a misperception as red, white and black. Black refers to the darkness of evening twilight; white, to the partial light of twilight (If you hadn't seen the rope, you never would have mistaken it for a snake.), and red, to the fact that the perception was colored by imagination. They also referred to these three aspects as the three Gunas (*Tamas, Rajas and Sattva*).

The mistake of seeing the underlying existence in time and space they called Maya or Prakriti, the first cause, and it is said to be made of these three Gunas. Tamas is said to have the veiling power. Rajas is said to have the projecting power. And Sattva is said to have the revealing power. (The veiling and projecting powers are presumably native to the genetic programming, but the revealing power, which is important to our physics, is native to sentiency itself.)

To quote the *Panchamahabhuta Sutras*, "*As if, being hidden, through the veiling power of Tamas, the nature of Brahman, through the revealing power of Sattva, shone in the otherness for which, through the projecting power of Rajas, it is, as it were, mistaken.*" What we see as energy is the result of this mistake, because the underlying existence (the changeless, the infinite, the undivided) must show through in what we see.

The concept of energy did not arise in European physics till 1845 with Thomas Young, but those older physicists saw that the whole Universe is made out of energy which they called *Shakti*. According to them, energy is that underlying Existence, which they called *Brahman*, as seen in time and space. And they could see that Existence has to be changeless, has to be infinite, has to be undivided, and that it has to show through in our physics.

According to the Vedantins, the first cause of our physics is *Vivarta*, apparition. It is the mistake of seeing the underlying existence as in time and space. After that, things proceed by *Parinama*, transformational causation, because the underlying existence shows through in the mistake as energy, as gravity, electricity and inertia, which cause the transformations. Parinama is what we European physicists usually think of as causation. It is governed by the conservation laws. The form of the energy may change but the amount of energy, in any such change, does not change. The electrical energy of an electrical particle would go to zero if, and only if, the size of that particle went to infinity, and the gravitational energy of the Universe would go to zero if, and only if, the dividedness of the Universe went to zero. (Infinity and undividedness are written into our physics. And changelessness is written in as inertia.)

Had those old physicists known what we know now, that the Universe is made of hydrogen and that the hydrogen is made of electrons and protons, they would have seen that the changeless shows through in the hydrogen as its inertia; the infinite, as its electricity; and the undivided, as its gravity and the attraction between opposites. Richard Feynman has pointed out that although we (in Europe) know how things fall, we have no knowledge of why they fall, and that although we know how things coast, we have no knowledge of why they coast. Einstein has made a similar remark about electricity, namely, that we cannot comprehend, on theoretical grounds, why matter appears as discrete electrical particles. Those older physicists knew why.

Only the primordial hydrogen arises by Vivarta from the changeless, the infinite, the undivided showing through in time and space. Everything else that we see arises from that hydrogen by Parinama. And the details are in Burbidge, Burbidge, Fowler and Hoyle, *Synthesis of the Elements in Stars*. We know now that the hydrogen falls together by transformational causation to galaxies and stars, planets and people. Even the bodies of living organisms arise by transformational causation, but the notion that one is such a body is, again, a Vivarta, a personal mistake.

The practices of the Advaita Vedantins take all this old physics for granted. It is even taken for granted that there is but one Reality behind both the individual and the Universe — *Ayam Atma Brahma* — this Atman is Brahman. (Atman is the reality behind the ego, and Brahman is the reality behind the Universe.) And it is taken for granted that if seeing it thus is a mistake, it must be possible to see through it; that it must be possible to see through the ego to the Atman, and through the Universe to Brahman.

Now those old Vedantins were not content simply to understand all this in their intellects. When they discovered that there must be an existence underlying the world which we see, their question was, "Can we reach it?" That was the effort that swept India in those days, and may yet sweep Europe and America. And that is why we have the Upanishads with all those stirring declarations.

All this is Brahman.
Let a man meditate on that visible world
as beginning, ending and breathing in Brahman.

That which is beyond this world
is without form and without suffering.
Those who know it become immortal.

I know that great Purusha
of sun-like luster beyond the darkness.
A man who knows Him truly passes over death.

Only when men shall roll up the sky like a hide
will there be an end of misery unless
"That" has first been known.

But still, for us physicists, there is a question. Why is that underlying existence seen as hydrogen? Perhaps those older physicists would have pointed out that in order to see, in space and time, that which is not in space and time, there is a problem. If the one were to be seen as two, the undividedness showing through, would bring the two together. What could stop it? Similarly, if the one were to be seen as many, the undividedness, showing through, would bring the manyness together. But if the one were to be seen as a duality within a plurality, as we see it in hydrogen, then the plurality could keep the duality up, and the duality could keep the plurality up, because neither can be seen alone. This would not be interesting, of course, if it didn't show up this way in our physics, but it does.

What we see in this Universe is an electrical duality (the electrons and the protons of the hydrogen atoms) against a gravitational plurality (the dispersion of the atoms through space). And the undividedness shows through as gravity (in the plurality) and as the attraction between plus and minus (in the duality). But the collapse of the electrical duality in the hydrogen atom is prevented by Heisenberg's uncertainty principle, because the proton is involved in the gravitational plurality and the electron is not. And the collapse of the gravitational plurality is prevented by Pauli's exclusion principle, because the neutrons have only one half of a spin duality. Heisenberg's uncertainty principle does not prevent the collapse of the duality of the electron and the positron (an electron with a positive charge) because gravity is not involved in the rest energy of either particle. But it does prevent the collapse of the electrical duality in the hydrogen atom because the rest energy of the proton is related to its gravitational separation from all the rest of the matter in the observable Universe. As Richard Feynman has pointed out, *"The electron is purely electrical; the proton is not."*

And Pauli's exclusion principle does not prevent Bose particles (without the spin duality) from sitting together.

The spiritual practices of the Advaita Vedantins follow the cosmology of those old physicists. If we have mistaken the real for the make-believe, there are four things to do about it. First, discriminate between the real and the make-believe! That's Jnana Yoga, the path of knowledge. Next, hang onto the real! That's Bhakti Yoga, the path of devotion — fall in love with the underlying existence! Next, give up the make-believe! Give up the attachment to the fruits of your actions! Give up the expectation that through transformational causation you'll reach the underlying existence! That's Karma Yoga, the path of action. And, finally, keep your body and mind in such fantastic shape that you can get the job done! That's Raja Yoga, the royal path.

Sri Ramakrishna saw the underlying existence, manifest in time and space, as Mother, and said that we are not the doers. Mother is the doer. And Lao Tzu said, *"To Her only I bow, trusting Her now and forever."*

Mother is the hydrogen. Mother is the star.
She falls it all together to make us what we are.
She makes the heavy elements and throws them all around,
To make the rocky planets with soil on the ground.
She scatters the ingredients across the planet Earth,
Assembling them with sunlight to give us all our birth.
She shines the sun on all these plants; the oxygen is waste.
We munch the plants, huff and puff, and run around in haste.
But we, poor dears, so mean of heart, assume we're in the know,
And thinking we can manage, fail to see Who runs the show.

John Dobson received his degree in chemistry from UC Berkeley in 1934 and served in the Ramakrishna Order as a monk for two decades, during which he acquired a love of service through astronomy. Creator of the Dobsonian telescope mount and founder of Sidewalk Astronomers, he passed away at 95 on Jan. 15th, 2014   www.sidewalkastronomers.com

◆ *Swami Aseshananda*

ETHICS & SPIRITUALITY
Dharma Fulfills Morality

On the 14th of June, 1987, Swami Aseshanandaji Maharaj gave out this transmission of Vedantic wisdom to all present, citing its salient differences from the ethics of dualistically-based religion and its relative aims.

The subject of my talk is ethics and spirituality. The West has accepted the philosophy of dualism. There is this theological dualism given by Augustine, and by Thomas Aquinas, that creature and Creator must be distinct. There is also ethical dualism given by Zoroastrianism. Christianity has borrowed its theological spectrum from the Jews, and has accepted morals and values of life from the Zoroastrians. And that is why we find in Mathew Arnold's texts on religion this morality touched with emotion. But the architects of American civilization, which is known mainly as a Protestant civilization, are Martin Luther and Calvin. Martin Luther has given morality but rejected renunciation. Calvin has given to the Americans a great pride; the pride of an affluent society. Further, America today has accepted conservatism as the philosophy of life. In order to be conservative you have to go back to your Puritanical heritage. And if you think in terms of Puritanical heritage you will have to think in terms of a literal interpretation of the Bible — that Christ is the only savior, and that he has come to redeem the sins of mankind. But he came to shed the eternal Light and show the way, not to condemn or focus on sin.

Swami Vivekananda came to America first in 1893. He did not accept Luther's rejection of renunciation. He did not accept the affluent society conclusion championed by Calvin. He came to represent the East and its focus on renunciation as the way — a renunciation that Christ also accepted. To represent the East you have to accept renunciation. Renunciation of what? Renunciation of your personal ego. Your personal self is finite! As long as you keep to this finite self, you are a prisoner of time. And in order to reach the goal of *jivanmukti*, or immortality, you have to transcend time; you also have to transcend history and, in turn, you will have to transcend ethical dualism. You also have to transcend intellectual pride and glory given by the two great philosophers of Greece, Plato and Aristotle.

The Leaky Boat of Western Thinking

The boat of Western civilization has sprung a leak. By the word "leak" I mean a great paradox. The paradox is that you want to reach the goal of perfection but you find it is impossible. Why it is impossible? Because you have accepted the world to be real. When you accept the world to be real you also accept your finite self to be real. When you accept the finite self to be real, you have to accept the Augustinian view of time — that time has a beginning and time has an end. Then, when there is an end of time, there will be a second coming of Christ and everything will be fine in this world. But nothing is ever fine about the unreal.

Interestingly, by contrast, when you take up Eastern thought you will find that it is not concerned with sin and salvation. Salvation suggests a post-mortem experience. When you attain salvation according to Paul you will get a new body. Salvation is interpreted by Paul as a resurrection. Resurrection is to be interpreted as a post-mortem emancipation. Here, you will not accept jivanmukti — that you can attain liberation in this life. In the East, especially in India, in order to attain true liberation you have to make a distinction between the apparent self which belongs to time, and the real Self which is timeless. The true Self, Atman, is actually the witness to the drama of life, and therefore we have to practice detachment to realize It. As they say nowadays, "Be in the world but not of the world." The world is created by your attachment to the sensate things of life. In order to reach the goal of freedom, the goal of perfection, we must transcend the world of time, space, and causation.

Now, Einstein has, from his scientific investigation, declared time and space to be relative. Thus, he did not accept Augustine's view of time; that time has a beginning and time has an end. He knew time and space to be relative, but he did not accept the law of causation to be relative; that was Heisenberg. But Heisenberg was not an illumined soul. An illumined soul is the likes of Gaudapada, Nagarjuna, and Shankara. And in this day and time it is Swami Vivekananda. None of these fell victim to the allures of the world of relativity.

Now, time is relative to our intellectual frame of reference; that has been explained by the German philosopher, Kant. He saw it as a category of the mind. He was basically a skeptic. Kant said that the thing itself, or the reality of God, will remain unknown and unknowable so long as one remains limited within the spectrum of the intellect and reason — the dualistic frame of reference.

A Christ comes to lift our Consciousness from the intellectual frame of reference to the spiritual frame. When you fall under the influence of time, space, and causation according to Shankara, it is called *maya*. And maya has its home based in the ego. If you have egocentric consciousness, you are bound to belong to time, and then the fear of death must come to you. And that is the reason Vedanta speaks in terms of *avidya*, root ignorance, instead of sin. We have no word sin in India, but we have the word avidya. It is simply the forgetfulness of our real nature.

And that is why Swami Vivekananda, when he opened his mouth in the West, especially in America at the Parliament of Religions, stated: *"Ye divinities on earth, it is a sin to call a man a sinner."* You are divine. But can you attain divinity? Not by accepting the *bhoga marga*, which is the path of enjoyment alone.

And that is the reason why I can say that Martin Luther, as well as Calvin, have both baptized the path of the bhoga marga and sanctified the ideal of an affluent society. This has given the Western man a great pride and so-called "honor," leading to acts such as splitting the atom and creating a hydrogen bomb for the destruction of the whole world and domination of other races.

Now, Sri Ramakrishna, by His very presence on earth, was trying to stem the tide of Western civilization. This Western civilization may be humanistic, and it may be ethical, but it has accepted materialism to be the keynote of the philosophy of life. There is no difference between the subhuman species and the human species if self-control does not become the purpose of life for the individual. And that was what Christ preached. Original Christianity was based on renunciation. Show me in the Bible any place where Christ has spoken about the reality of this world of time, space, and causation. Christ brought renunciation in order to attain realization of God in a higher state of consciousness. When I was a student of the St. Paul's Cathedral Mission College, it was Christ who attracted me to spiritual life. And it is Christ who instilled in my mind that the key to the solution of all problems of life and death is renunciation. Renunciation of what? Renunciation of the false God that you are worshipping. The "false God" is your own ego whom you say speaks to you as the voice of God. That is why Sri Ramakrishna taught his disciples: *"All troubles will cease when ego dies."* That is the reason why when I see a cross it signals to me to cross this ego off my list. Then you can lead a life of divinity, a life of immortality, a life of perfection, a life of certainty, and a life of conferring blessings to all of mankind, not just to your own nation.

Good and Bad Acts of Stupifaction

Doing good to the world, or going about and doing good; this is the philosophy of humanism. But have you noticed? It only ends in going about and making matters worse. Can you do good to any person unless you do good to yourself first? Can you issue a check of say, $50,000, if you have not stored up that amount in the bank? Therefore, *sadhana* is necessary — spiritual self-effort from the cradle to the grave. Teach your children self-discipline, not self-expression. Self-expression here in a materialistic society means sense-expression, and sense-expression means slavery to the soul. Therefore, never give freedom to the senses; get freedom from the senses. Watch your senses. Regulate your senses. And also be a master of your senses. In other words, if you live on the emotional plane, you are not riding the horse, the horse is riding you.

I will give you an example. A holy man, a *sadhu*, was making a pilgrimage to Kedarnath. After covering some distance, long distances, he became tired. He thought, "If I had a pony, a horse, then it would give me tremendous relief; I need a horse. So he prayed to God, "Oh God, please help me. Please give me horse." At that moment, the Prince of that state was going about with his retinue. The Commander in Chief, who was the leader of the group, found that his mare had given birth to a young colt. Then he told his servant, "I have heard of that man who wants a horse. Bring him to me." When the holy man arrived, the commander ordered him, saying, "Carry that horse! Carry it on your shoulders!" So he got the horse, no doubt — not to ride, but to carry on the shoulders.

Similarly, there is this bhoga marga, or path of enjoyment. You think that you'll be happy, but happiness never comes. Why? Nachiketas says in the *Katho Upanisad,* that happiness never comes through the sensate things of life, so free yourself from attachment to sense objects. Nachiketas had spiritual awakening via renunciation. You see, enjoyment saps the vigor of the senses. I want to know the Truth which will make me free.

And what is that Truth then? Just ask "Who am I?" And the answer to "Who am I" comes through *samadhi.* When you reach a higher state of consciousness, which is timeless, you will realize "I am not finite but infinite; I am not imperfect, but perfect; I am not sinful, I am Divine." You have only hypnotized yourself into thinking that you are a man or a woman, a Hindu or a Christian, an Eastern man or a Western man, and so forth.

Vedanta Speaks Truth

Vedanta speaks in terms not of ethical humanism, but rather in terms of the universal experience of man when he has realized that Atman and Brahman are identical. When we renounce our attachment to our psycho-physical being, we enter into the heart of reality which is *Satchitananda* — existence infinite, knowledge infinite, bliss infinite. But as long as we remain on the intellectual plane of existence we only identify ourselves with *nama-rupa*; that means name and form. When we identify with name and form we are like waves floating on the surface of an eternal ocean.

And that is what Christ said to the Samaritan woman. One day Christ was very thirsty. He did not go to a fountain, but he went to a well. In those days there was no faucet but wells were there. In India I used to go to the orphanage in Benares where I knew these certain wells were very good, and had clean water, and also our water here in our own retreat center near St. Helens is very good water, 99% pure — because in the world of maya you cannot have 100% purity. [laughter]

So anyway, Christ went to the well and the Samaritan woman was drawing water. "Would you kindly give some water

> "Calvin's philosophy was to pray but keep the powder keg dry. That means your faith in God is provisional so you have to back it up with "gun power." That is the reason why America thinks in terms of star wars. But star wars will not help; 'Vanity of vanities, all this is vanity.' How many civilizations have come, have gone. Where is this Greek civilization today? Where is the Roman civilization? Where is the Egyptian civilization? Where is the Assyrian civilization? These were the civilizations of Maya! All these civilizations have come and disappeared."

to me, He asked?" She looked up and saw a tall figure, majestic eyes, sparkling face. She immediately understood that he was a high class Hebrew. In Christ's time the Hebrews looked down upon the Samaritans. It is something like hill-billy people. [laughter] In this country, if you ask who are the Brahmins in America, they will answer "….those who live in Boston or New England." Why? Because the pilgrim fathers came to Cape Cod on the ship, Mayflower. I went there once to see.

So, the pilgrim fathers came on the Mayflower, but they brought what is called Puritanism. And their great achievement is the University. Their University was 355 years old. At first it was a Bible school. They followed Calvin because Luther was an emotional person, while Calvin was very ethical and very sober, very intellectual. As I said, he had given the heart of the organization and the will to build an affluent society and free education. But every person must go to church, must belong to the church. Calvin's philosophy was to pray but keep the powder keg dry. That means your faith in God is provisional so you have to back it up with "gun power." That is the reason why America thinks in terms of star wars. But star wars will not help; "Vanity of vanities, all this is vanity." How many civilizations have come, have gone. Where is this Greek civilization today? Where is the Roman civilization? Where is the Egyptian civilization? Where is the Assyrian civilization? These were the civilizations of Maya! All these civilizations have come and disappeared. That is why Christ advised not to build your house on sand, but build your house on a rock. And that rock is not Faith alone; that rock is the Atman, your real Self — which is not finite but infinite; which is not mortal but immortal; which does not go to heaven; which does not even know reincarnation. Birth, death, and rebirth belong to the *ajnanis*, not to the *Jnanis*.

But a man — when he becomes illumined, when he becomes a jnani, *aham brahmasmi* — he realizes that he is existence infinite, knowledge infinite, and bliss infinite. That is your *svarupa*, that is your real essence. And your svarupa lives on; your real nature is like the sun whose nature is to shine. But for many days in this city of Portland, you do not have the vision of the sun [laughter]. That does not mean the sun does not exist; it has only been covered up by clouds. If the sun disappeared there would come the dissolution of the solar system.

One time, you see, I was taking a swami from Portland to San Francisco. The trip started with rain and ended with rain as long as we were in Oregon. But when we crossed the Oregon border, there was the beautiful sunshine at Mt. Shasta. Similarly, a sun does not lose the power of shining. Just so, the real Self of mankind never loses the power of knowing the Truth which will make the human being free.

And therefore, our philosophy is not the religion of dualism, but the philosophy of nondualism, which speaks in terms of immortality of the Spirit, divinity of the Soul, and the universality of love and wisdom. It is therefore that Sri Ramakrishna has given a message. That message is to never "preach" religion. Religion should not be preached. Religion is to be lived. In its own beautiful way it is like a lotus. When the lotus is not in bloom, bees will never come. But when the lotus fully blossoms, it never sends out any advertisement. The Lotus of Self Realization has no public media. There's no television channel for it. There's no radio station. There's no Time magazine or Life magazine to report on it. Well, Life magazine is no longer in existence [laughter]. But Time magazine is still in existence. But as I was saying, if you live in time you are bound to think in terms of the predominance of life and the acceptance of death to be the final destiny of man. Therefore, try to reach a state of consciousness which is timeless. When you are timeless you will also be deathless. And when you are deathless you must be changeless as well. And when you are changeless you will be immortal. If you are immortal then you are infinite.

Infinite East, Finite West

And that is the main difference between the Eastern and Western man. The former thinks in terms of his infinite nature, while the latter thinks in terms of his finite nature. But one's true nature is not a speculative idea. Your infinite nature is not just a theme of philosophy, nor is It just an article of faith; It is a divine experience. The classic example of this experience in our times is Sri Ramakrishna, who has covered the gamut of spiritual experiences. As it were, He has declared to all human beings, "I have realized God as a Divine Incarnation. I have realized God as the *Antaryami* — the inner ruler immortal seated in the heart. I have realized God as the immortal Spirit — timeless, deathless, changeless and infinite. And man can also realize that Truth which will make him free."

Christ also realized *"I and my Father are One."* This "I" is not the historical Jesus; "I" is the *Atman*. And "Father" is not the personal God; "Father" is *Nirguna Brahman*, the Formless Essence. But the West has rejected Nirguna Brahman; the West has accepted only the personal God. The Western theologians always use "He" as the ultimate Cause. To them, He is the Cause of this universe. But Vedanta declares that Brahman is beyond cause and effect. It is also beyond gender. And they say about

> "....one's true nature is not a speculative idea. Your infinite nature is not just a theme of philosophy, nor is It just an article of faith; It is a divine experience. The classic example of this experience in our times is Sri Ramakrishna, who has covered the gamut of spiritual experiences. He is saying to human beings, "I have realized God as a divine incarnation. I have realized God as the Antaryami — the inner ruler immortal seated in the heart. I have realized God as the immortal Spirit — timeless, deathless, changeless, and infinite. And man can also realize that Truth...."

Christ, the Son, that he is a Divine Incarnation, and that He is the only one. That is finite thinking.

If you were to travel in a spaceship towards the sun, taking photographs along the way, it will look like a little orb in the beginning, but as you go higher and higher you will find the sun to be vast, spreading through space. Further, you will find that there are many suns in the night skies. That is infinite thinking.

Therefore, Swami Vivekananda use to say, it is not that God has created man in His image; my philosophy says it is man who creates God in his image. When you are body conscious, you must think of God as an extra cosmic deity, a *deus ex machina*. But when you develop spiritual consciousness, then you will say *"I am the vine, you are the branches."* That means a theistic view of life, that God is imminent and God is also transcendent. The West stops there. But when you attain *Nirvikalpa Samadhi,* you will say, like Sri Ramakrishna in his inimitable language, I cast off the form of the Mother and my mind soared into the Transcendental Beyond; I reached unlimited Consciousness where there is no duality, where there is no time, where there is no consciousness of changefulness.

But when Christ was talking to his disciples, those who were following the path of renunciation and meditation, he said, *"I am the vine, you are branches."* That means *Savikalpa Samadhi.* But to his closest disciples he said, *"I and my Father are One."* And also he gave an example of the *"Kingdom of Heaven."* He was talking spiritual matters and some children close by were making noise. His disciples told them to go away, but Christ put one of the children on his lap and he said, *"I was talking to you about the Kingdom of Heaven. You cannot enter the Kingdom of Heaven unless you be like a little child."* This means you must possess childlike innocence, childlike purity, childlike sincerity, and childlike dependence upon God. Although Christ spoke about dependence upon God, he also spoke about the Oneness of God. You see, when you depend upon God, God is personal. But when you become One with God, God is impersonal. Therefore, to me, an Avatar comes to build a bridge between the personal God and the impersonal God.

Avatar as an Exemplar, not a Savior

An Avatar never dies. Death is bound to come to an individual soul, but the glory of an Avatar, a Divine Incarnation, is that he remains as the indwelling Spirit even after the death of the body and ego. He is then an exemplar who is to be realized by his devotees — those who long for the vision of God as a drowning man longs for a breath of air.

The Avatar's message is that in order to reach purity of heart, renunciation is necessary. The method is there, the goal is also there. The goal is not salvation. I would change that word salvation to perfection. It was Paul who introduced the word salvation. Sin and salvation, both ideas were the dubious gift of Paul. The letters of Paul are the commentaries of the Bible. And all the theologians have accepted them — Augustine, Thomas Aquinas, etc.

Faith and Reason at Odds in the West

In present times when Swami Vivekananda came to the West, there existed a conflict between reason and faith. Faith had been accepted by Augustine; salvation only through faith. But Thomas Aquinas, because he was a philosopher, and through his brilliant intellect, tried to prove the existence of God. There are his five proofs for the existence of God. When I was studying philosophy I had to read them. They are things like ontological proof, theological proof, cosmological proof. What are these things? These are mere inference. Just as you see smoke, so you have to think that there must be fire, similarly, when you see that the world is not a chaos but a cosmos, then you think that there must be an intelligent Cosmic Being behind this universe. This was introduced to Thomas Aquinas by Aristotle, called the Unmoved Mover. God is infinite, but He is the Ultimate Cause of this universe as well. And it is He who has brought this universe into being. He is imminent in this universe, and also Transcendent beyond it. This is called a theological interpretation.

But a scientific frame of reference does not think in terms of causation to be final. This was true of Heisenberg especially. Einstein accepted causation to be final. Therefore, Protestant Christianity, to me, is a revised and enlarged addition to Judaism because it emphasizes the reality of God, the reality of family life, the reality of society, and the reality of a nation. The difference between Catholicism and Protestantism is that Catholicism thinks in terms of the infallible Church. But Protestantism thinks in terms of glory, power, beauty, grandeur, and ethical supremacy of the nation. That is the reason why any American who becomes an astronaut and goes to the moon will plant the Star Spangled Banner there [chuckle]. That is good; the glory is there. You see, pride is necessary. But in order to be spiritual you have to become universal. Therefore, I like conservatism, you see. It gives pride, honor, dignity, and also ethical living and hard work. Puritanism will not allow you to sleep or go into debt. Puritanism will tell you to seek first the Kingdom of

Heaven and everything else will be added unto you. "Everything else" means personal jet plane, ten million dollars, and a mansion [laughter]. And what of the congregation? They are working class people; they will get vicarious satisfaction [laughter].

This "I, me, and mine" must go, you see. The little I and me connected with anything which is finite, which is changeful, which is precarious, and which is uncertain, must go. I and mine should be connected with Thou and Thine. Thou and Thine will help the individual to be spiritual. Spiritual means not going towards the periphery, but going towards the center.

Serious Ethics and Ethical Humor

So now I'm talking about ethics. Ethics must be used as a means to an end. The end should be oneness of existence, solidarity of the universe, divinity of man, and immortality of the soul. I want to conquer death. In order to conquer death I will have to go into samadhi, to reach a higher state of consciousness. Then you can really say *"Death, where is thy sting? Grave, where is thy victory?"* and mean it; not just mouth it in a play.

Death belongs to ignorant people. An illumined soul does not die. We call that *Mahasamadhi*. If I am to interpret Christ, I will say, on the cross he entered into Mahasamadhi. That means he identified himself with Nirguna Brahman. First when he said *"Let this cup pass away,"* he wanted to live. But he had a vision of his Heavenly Father. That means Savikalpa Samadhi. He said, *"To Thy hand I commend my Spirit."* Then he went to Nirvikalpa Samadhi. Christ can be seen today. Sri Ramakrishna saw Christ. Therefore, we do not preach the avatarhood of Sri Ramakrishna for a simple reason. The acceptance of Avatar must change the life of the individual. That is what Christ also said. He said, *"Know them by their fruits."*

My ethics theme has become a little austere and grave, so let me talk in a lighter manner. One time, after arriving here in America, and when I was in Trabuco, I met brother Bill from Oklahoma. I think he bought Swami Prabhavananda's old car. The car gave him some trouble. So we took it to a garage and gave it to a mechanic. He began fixing it as we stood by. Soon, a bolt fell down at the mechanic's feet and he said, "Jesus Christ!" Later, a nut fell down under the car, and he cried, "Jesus!" Every time anything fell he said "Jesus Christ!" I turned to Bill and said, "He is a holy mechanic, we should hire him as our mechanic." [laughter] Bill told me, "Swami, you do not know. He is cursing." I was surprised and said, "How come?" Probably that is the reason it is said in the Bible, *"Do not repeat the name of the Lord in vain."*

For ethics to reach a positive end, first, transformation is necessary. Second comes edification. Third, is realization. Transformation only comes when we live an ethical life. Purity of life cannot come by acceptance of the bhoga marga, the path of pleasure. You must listen to the voice of the East — renounce, renounce, renounce. Buddha is a representative of the East. He said that anything you experience in the realm of time is filled with pain, is filled with the illusoriness of existence. Shankara called it maya. It is a mere appearance, a mere shadow. Plato spoke of the imagery of a cave, that intellectual life can give only shadowy pleasures.

For instance, America has accepted television. America should accept God vision. In television you externalize your senses. In God vision you internalize your senses. That means, withdraw your mind from the periphery! In order to see God you have to enter into your heart. Christ also said, *"When you pray, enter into the closet."* Here, "closet" means the cave of the heart. That cave will be effulgent with the light of the Spirit, and the realization of God through His grace will dawn on the horizon of your mind.

But Buddhism lays the stress on self-effort. Buddhism does not speak of Divine Grace. Take for example, when Buddha said to his favorite disciple, Ananda, when he was about to quit this world: *"Weep not Ananda; be a lamp unto yourself. Take no external refuge."* Christ on the cross said, *"To Thy hand I commend my Spirit. Thy will be done, not my will."* But Sri Ramakrishna wants to bring a synthesis. Human effort and the struggle for realization of God is necessary in order to come to the level of sattvic consciousness. In a sattvic plane of consciousness, the mind in the heart reflects divine Reality. This reflected joy will inspire the individual to discover and realize the infinite joy which comes from realization of God in Nirvikalpa Samadhi. And towards this purpose we must bend all our efforts, must scorn surface delights, live laborious days, and try to realize God in the consciousness of our soul, away from the din and bustle of the madding crowd.

Becoming in the West, Being in the East

There two types of meditation. The West has focused on the power of doing, but it should also accept the power of being. That is what you also find in Thomas Aquinas. He wrote the beautiful *Summas*, but on All Saint's Day he had a vision, probably a samadhi. Similarly, Sri Ramakrishna says that when one attains *Brahmajnana*, knowledge of the shastras will become like mere straw. We must transcend the world of maya and realize the world of eternal beauty, uncharted freedom, and perennial happiness. Only a man who has realized God in his own consciousness can be like a stream delivering the message of peace to the rest of the world, irrespective of creed, color, nationality, or race, because he has achieved the goal of life. And he now wants to distribute it to the rest of mankind by his shining example, by his pure character, by edifying vision, and by a sublime look, because he thinks of men not as men only, but as glorious children of the Divine Spirit. *"Hear ye children of immortality I have realized the Truth by crossing the bonds of maya. By knowing him alone, man crosses death and attains immortality here and now."*

So let America listen to the voice of Sri Ramakrishna, beautify its vision, ennoble its outlook, and be a blessing to mankind. America is supreme in scientific achievement, and therefore, America has a responsible task to perform by spiritualizing inner life and bringing forth a society which will not be merely affluent, but illumined — where *jivanmuktas* will play the part of distributing the wealth of spirituality to the rest of mankind. It may be a dream now, but let this dream come true through the blessing of God.

Now, they say, "the more the merrier." Therefore I request Dr. Lex Hixon to speak. He is a disciple of Swami Nikhilananda.

Lex Hixon: Because this platform is so powerful, really, any initiated person could stand here and feel the flow of spiritual teaching and illumination that flows from it. And Swami has been here in Portland for some 35 years, since 1955. And he's practiced absolute stability. He hasn't even gone back to visit India, as far as I know. And he's totally given himself to our culture, and to this specific spot in the world, which when our relations with China normalize, Portland could become a very, very important interface between Asia and the West. There is a meaning that the highest teachings are being given here; a meaning for the future of the culture. There is a kind of limited teaching that is distorting our cultural scene today. When those limited teachings come to Oregon, they're reduced and shown to be empty by the Swami. That sort of thing was seen recently here in Oregon with the horribly skewed drama of the Rajneeshpuram. So there is real power here in Portland at this center for the purification of the world, and today we're participating in it. And you might say it's flowing from the Essence of Reality. This photograph of Sri Ramakrishna behind me is a product of Western civilization in that we developed the photographic process, but this photograph is really a photograph of pure Essence.

So you might say that it is Essence transmitting through Essence to Essence. And this was precisely Ramakrishna's own experience when he entered the Kali temple. In his own words he said that everything — not only the image of the Divine Mother — but everything in the temple including the vessels, and even the marble door sills, were filled with Essence; were filled with this Supreme Consciousness. And maybe even the word "filled" is not adequate, because that might imply that there is something finite there which is being filled with the infinite. But really, the vessels themselves are this Supreme Consciousness, are this Essence.

So that's why it's such a privilege to stand here and say a few words, because one has the experience of Essence pouring through the vessel and being received by Essence. And the vessel itself is Essence. So what Swami calls *Atmajnan* or *Brahmajnan*, or the knowledge of the oneness of Atman and Brahman — all these statements from the Upanisadic language have to do with the fact that Essence is being poured into Essence.

And that is what is actually happening for us here and now. As Swami said, it's not a speculative doctrine; it's an experience. And although the swami stresses how demanding the road is, the preparation and purification that is needed to have this experience in its fullness, I'm actually convinced that everyone in this room, right now, is having this experience due to the grace of the situation. All of us are appreciating it on different levels, and we don't have to think, well, maybe if I sit in this room another 20 years, and listen to Swami speak another 20 years, then maybe I'll have realization; maybe I'll see then what he's talking about. This is not true. It is happening now.

But as Swami warned us, we should not be cocksure. Don't assume that Sri Ramakrishna has placed his blessing on your level of understanding. We always have to be cautious about self-deception. As Swami said, self-deception is the major problem in spiritual life. But at the same time there is such a thing as confidence; confidence in the *Mahavakyas* of the *Upanisads* that were given to the students by the teacher in early times — like *Tat twam asi, Thou art That*. And as I've said earlier, Sri Ramakrishna's mantra and Swami's very words are there to increase our confidence, not to make us weak and lacking in spiritual assurance. So, on one side there needs to be carefulness about self-deception, and on the other side a supreme confidence in the situation — that the full Essence of the Truth is being transmitted here and now. And that there is nothing lacking here. We could go to the finest ashram in India, we could go to Belur Math, we could go to Mecca, we could go any place in the world and not find a more complete spiritual situation as this. That kind of confidence is extremely necessary.

But confidence itself does not come from us; it also comes from Essence. It is something that's being provided. And it is so clear to me when I come to visit this ashram. It is not clear to me most of the time in my life, but there's a great clarity here and a powerful unveiling of the Truth as well. And I realize, just as in closing the other day, that when I meditate, let's say, in the living presence of Sri Ramakrishna in the shrine, I'm always thinking it would be nice if Sri Ramakrishna appeared to me and said something to me, maybe even just a few words [laughter], and I could be so proud of that. And for the rest of my life I could say, you know, he said something to me.

But then I realize this is absurd, in this way, because when Swami stands here and speaks for an hour and a half, this is Sri Ramakrishna, this is Essence saying to us precisely what It wants to say, playfully, and in terms of our own culture, with knowledge of our own foibles — not only our cultural foibles, but our personal foibles. So it is all fine-tuned to each of us. This is the meaning of *darshan*, and of the *guru*, and of the guidance of an illumined soul. It is not something coming from Swami Aseshananda as an individual, it is Essence pouring through Essence into Essence.

And if we do not have the confidence to live on the level of Essence ourselves, then we aren't receiving it. But the point is that the people who are stable here, and come again and again to be a part of the life of this ashram, they are on the level of Essence or they wouldn't be here still; they wouldn't savor the sweetness and the subtleness of place. Because as Swami said, the lotus, when it blossoms, has no media outreach, and it does not glorify itself. It is very simple. So as far as I can see there is no self-glorification whatsoever of this particular ashram, which is kind of rare — not only in the West but I would imagine in the East too. The temptation is always to glorify the lotus and to put signs around it and ribbons around it. But here, there is just this — the lotus is opened and the bees are attracted.

Sri Ramakrishna used to sing that beautiful hymn, that in the beginning the seeker is like the bee and God is like the lotus. But as spiritual life deepens, that God becomes the bee and the seeker is the lotus. So we are being sought by this Essence. And we are being found by the Essence, because the Essence never loses us. The Essence can never be veiled. You can never escape the Essence.

So here, that beautiful meeting is happening, and it is for, as Swami always ends his talk, the blessing of mankind. Because our very culture, as Swami said, what the West needs is a transfusion of this kind of knowledge of Oneness. And that is precisely what's happening in this little temple. This transfusion is going on and this is the mystery of why Swami Vivekananda came to the West in 1893. He was sent by Sri Ramakrishna; he was sent by Essence. And that was not a chance historical event. It was part of the unfolding of a global civilization. And what Swamiji did in this country and what the great swamis have done here in his name can never be reversed. It is extremely powerful and it is on a totally different plane from the popular spirituality of, say, the Rajneeshpuram, or other less legitimate kinds of practices. It's on the very deepest level of the culture because Sri Ramakrishna came to enliven and awaken the world in its fullest sense, in all its diversity. And Sri Ramakrishna came as a Bee seeking the lotus of the world, to pollinate it and to deify it.

As Swami has explained, the nature of Tantra, of the Tantric vision is to attain the perfect knowledge of Oneness and then to deify all the manifestations of Oneness. This is the glorious future for humanity that we see unfolding. And Swami ended his talk with this, like Martin Luther King was saying — I have a dream. Now, Swami was saying, this may be a dream, but let's realize it.

There is no doubt that this glory of true humanity has always been true. Our lives are to be led not for our own personal salvation, or our own personal escape from the problems, or transcending everything. Our personal lives are to be lived for the enlivening and awakening of all mankind. This is one of the fundamental vows that the monks of the Ramakrishna Order take, and is one of the fundamental vows that all of us who are initiated into Sri Ramakrishna take. It is for all humanity, not for ourselves; it is not just for our own personal spiritual evolution.

But as Swami says, it comes through; it is for our own liberation and for the liberation of the world that we have to do good to ourselves, in order to transmit these blessings to humanity. I think of Swami Vivekananda's vision of Sri Ramakrishna as being like the Ganges springing up spontaneously, right in the streets. And all its holy water is flooding outwards, and Swamiji took it and is distributing it.

So this Essence is so abundant, so generously flowing to all of us, and we can distribute it. But that doesn't mean that we have to go into the streets of Portland with little pamphlets about the Vedanta Center and string pictures of our guru around our necks. It is an inner experience. Each one of our breaths is a distribution of Essence to all, not only to humanity, but to all of creation.

We have found two hundred billion galaxies now, and we're still counting. But what we think of as the planetary existence extends perhaps infinitely. But it is all One, it is all the unity of Existence. Therefore, we're touching it now, all of it. And if we are shining this light of Essence, we are touching all of it. Thank you very much.

Swami: Yes, good. A mother never refuses to give the best to her children, so give — like the Holy Mother did. And now there will be prasad while I chant from the Gita:

(Gita Chanting and distribution of prasad)

And now for a few announcements. We are very pleased to have guests from New York and Hawaii. Some of them have left, and two will go tomorrow. It shows that Sri Ramakrishna's family is not only those people who live in Portland, Oregon. There's a big family, you see. Wherever we look, the centers are there. And there are some centers which are not officially affiliated, they are also our groups. Anyway, there are two centers in New York. Those devotees who belong to those centers, when they come here, we feel happy, because Sri Ramakrishna belongs not to a particular state, like Oregon. Somebody said that it is the edge of the world, it is not the edge. [laughter] It is going its own way. Others are just devotees in a bigger city, that is all. And business people go there, but living is very costly. Here, we can say we have got nature. We have got the ocean which represents the Divine Mother — always moving, always doing something good — and the mountain, like Mt. Hood.

So you see, the ocean represents the Divine Mother — very active, doing good to humanity. And the mountain represents calmness which comes from meditation. One represents the active West, the other is the contemplative East. And through contemplation they will transcend time, transcend this world of relativity. So here, nature is very propitious to the people so as to awaken their spiritual consciousness. Hold fast to the Divine Mother for inspiration and activity, and to the Lord or Divine Father for attainment of calmness of mind. Intense activity combined with intense calmness will bring our cherished goal during this sojourn on this earth, which is like a pilgrimage. The end of all pilgrimages is realization of God in the sanctuary of the soul.

Swami Aseshananda, a direct disciple of Sri Sarada Devi, Sri Ramakrishna's wife and spiritual consort, was the Spiritual Minister of the Vedanta Society of Portland for over forty years. He also received holy company with some of the direct disciples of the Great Master. He is the author of *Glimpses of a Great Soul*, on the life and teachings of Swami Saradananda.

ZEN PRINCIPLES & DISTRACTIONS
Mayoi – Avoiding Errors on the Dharmic Path

In Lex Hixon's beautiful book on Zen Buddhism, entitled *Living Buddha Zen*, he points out that Mother India accomplished a fifty-two generation march from the time of Shakyamuni Buddha to her present perch in Japan, carrying with her the profound teachings of the eternal dharma. Buddha dharma thus lived for twenty-eight generations in India, passed into China and thrived there for twenty-two generations, then began its recent life-phase in Japan that is presently two generations old. This salient fact of history explains the unmistakable Indian flavor and atmosphere that infuses Zen Buddhism, indicating as well its close similarity with Hindu darshanas such as Yoga and Advaita Vedanta.

The Five Vehicles or Types of Zen

Refreshingly candid, Zen Buddhism refuses compromise much like a lotus leaf sheds water. As the accompanying chart on the following page shows, a beginner on the path of Zen is apt to enter the gate via *Bonpo Zen*, becoming preoccupied with health in much the same way that present day hatha practitioners are doing. Fixating on body and brain rather than mind and spirit, many wander off the path, disillusioned by their own short-sightedness.

There is another gateway that presents itself to the beginner early on as well, called *Gedo Zen*. Practitioners here are assuming that, in the name of some immature eclecticism or universality, they can practice the precepts and teachings of Zen while simultaneously entertaining teachings from other traditions. Unless and until this orientation is corrected, the famous "one-taste bowl" experience leading to the perfect innate sense of Enlightenment free of admixtures can never dawn on the mind.

In *Shojo Zen*, a small vehicle is granted the seeker. The focus here is a still underdeveloped idea in the mind of the seeker that the goal of life is to escape from cycles of rebirth. Though this is an important phase in spiritual practice wherein latent karmas get exposed and expunged, greater realization is still in store for the sincere aspirant.

Daijo Zen is the "great vehicle" of Zen practice. It observes the intrinsic unity of all things, even right into the everyday life of average beings in the world. It is only surpassed by the "Supreme Vehicle" called *Saijojo Zen*, where the famous arrival of the integration of way, path, and goal prevails.

Eight Famous Distractions in Zen Practice

With these five stages and their corresponding vehicles — inferior to superior — in mind, the dedicated Zen practitioner can more easily watch out for the many distractions that are bound to rise up along the pathway. One of the most prominent of these is the imposition of *Buji Zen*. Much like in Advaita Vedanta, with its declaration of *Mahavakyas* that proclaim the absolute identity of the individual soul (*jivatman*) with the Supreme Soul (*Paramatman*), an early disclosure of the presence of Buddha Nature (*Bussho*) within the practitioner can give way to a premature assumption of Enlightenment. This plays havoc with the need for spiritual practice, for the foolish seeker lamely concludes that he/she is already enlightened — even when feet have barely been set on the path!

One of the signs of such deceit in a beginner is an outflow of words that are mere repetition of what has been heard or read from masters and scripture. This form of pretense has a name as well, called *Yako Zen*. True realization of the marvelous dharma and its workings is still absent in such minds.

Buji Zen and Yako Zen may be likened to a sort of "dating period" with actual Zen, where many wrong moves and much clumsiness are involved. Many of the impositions to follow emerge out of such early incompetence, especially when the lack of a Zen Master, or *Roshi*, is concerned. Both *Zembhyo* and *Bonno* represent fitting examples here. Zembhyo is "Zen Sickness." It inflicts practitioners who still have to encounter their emotional body and all the internal impressions lurking there. This is where the seeker finds out that thoughts are not the only problem in meditation, but that feelings, emotions, sensations, imagination, and brooding all figure into the puzzle. Along with this melange of undesirables comes another set of insinuations in a dubious form termed Bonno. Worldliness ranks high in this league of interlopers, followed by those all-too-familiar six passions, the desires that foster them, and the suffering that follows them. These proceed from a false reading of the world, which is why a competent spiritual guide is necessary so that otherwise insurmountable differences can be reconciled.

A case in point here is that imposition Zen masters call *Makyo*, or "diabolical phenomena." The negativities of the world are legion enough without the mind dwelling on them and turning them into veritable hallucinations. The mind is a delicate mechanism, and treating it carefully is a crucial part of Zen practice. The advice of the master is to be followed so that such abberations can be avoided. However, there is also what is termed *Katto*, which translates as "thicket of creeping vines." Too much verbiage is not good, what to speak of failing to extract from wise words their essential meaning.

Finally there are two obstacles that occur at a more advanced level. They are *Goseki* and *Hasan*. Goseki can be recognized in those who cling to a few early spiritual experiences. Instead of moving on to plunge deeper they remain at the surface level. Hasan brings forward authentic enlightenment experiences, long-awaited, but its imposition manifests as an "interruption" in one's practice that needs to be ongoing in order to achieve higher and better levels of enlightenment.

This brief list of known distractions stand in the way of the natural state of awareness evinced by such profound words as *Bussho, Gedatsu, Ku, Shunya,* and *Satori*. Using exquisite care and gradual progress one's Buddha Nature can be duly realized.

Zen Principles & Distractions
Mayoi – Avoiding Errors on the Dharmic Pathway

"The Goal of Zen is Bussho, consciously living in one's Imminent Nature, which is devoid of mass, beyond individuality and personality, and outside the realm of imagination — synonymous with Shunyata."

Five Types of Zen

Bonpo Zen - Unenlightened person practicing Zen for bodily & mental health
Gedo Zen - "Outside Way," mixing Zen with teachings of other traditions
Shojo Zen - "Small Vehicle," mainly seeks discontinuation of rebirth in cycles
Daijo Zen - "Great Vehicle," observes the unity of all things, & Zen in everyday life
Saijojo Zen - "Supreme Vehicle," where way, path, and goal are all fused in one

Buji Zen - A light and immature attitude towards the teachings wherein practitioners think that since they are already Buddha nature, they do not have to do practice or seek enlightenment.

Yako Zen - "Wild Fox Zen," inflicting those who pretend to be enlightened but really only mouth the teachings, having no deep or true realization of the dharma whatsoever.

Hasan - Interruption of Zen practice by an enlightenment experience — celebrated but not stressed — that keeps the aspirant from gaining many more and higher profound experiences.

Bussho - Gedatsu - Ku - Shunya - Satori

Goseki - "Trace of Enlightenment," sticking to those practitioners who cling to their initial insight experiences instead of living as if oblivious to their own enlightenment — in a natural way.

Zembyo - "Zen sickness," which make up the host of distracting thoughts, feelings, emotions, sensations, appearances and broodings that arise during the course of a student's practice of Zen.

Makyo - "Diabolical phenomena," like the negative circumstances of the ordinary world, which the practitioner should not entertain in the mind, letting them turn into mental hallucinations.

Bonno - Worldliness, sensuality, passions, longings, suffering, and misery, all rising from a false view of the world.

"The sun shines by day, and the moon by night; the Warrior is resplendent in armor and the Brahman radiant in meditation. But Buddha, the Awakened One, illumines both day and night by the splendor of His wisdom."
Dhammapada

Katto - "Thicket of creeping vines" meaning falling victim to hearing too many words while failing to take the essence from them.

Chart by Babaji Bob Kindler, Property of SRV Associates

NECTAR BOOK REVIEWS

Sri Sarada Devi and Her Divine Play
by Swami Chetanananda
Vedanta Society of St Louis, 2015
Paperback, 876 pgs, illustrated

Sri Sarada Devi and Her Divine Play immerses the reader in *Liladhyan*, meditation on the Divine Sport of an incarnation of God. This practice unerringly strengthens devotion and faith by awakening the divine Presence within one's heart.

In his fine preface, Swami Chetanananda writes: "After translating Swami Saradananda's *Sri Ramakrishna Lilaprasangha (Sri Ramakrishna and His Divine Play)*, I felt my work was half done. Just as a theatre audience becomes irritated and begins shouting if an interesting drama ends midway, so I thought the devoted followers of Ramakrishna and Holy Mother might be annoyed with me if I did not complete the whole drama."

Personally, I had not realized how much I had been yearning for a book such as this on the Holy Mother, Sri Sarada Devi, nor had I considered that one was even possible. The author has compiled an excellent selection of excerpts from previous biographies and reminiscences, exquisitely cast in a fresh setting to highlight important themes. Then, he has filled out the Mother's life with an abundance of enthralling new stories and teachings translated from Bengali, relying primarily on eye-witness accounts. In this book of 876 absorbing pages, Swami Chetanananda skillfully performs the duty of a *sutradhara*, one who keeps the thread of the story clearly presented, by writing introductions, commentaries, and elucidations so the reader will extract the most from Sri Sarada Devi's life. Frankly speaking, a book like this is not to be reviewed, but revered.

For those who are not acquainted with Sri Sarada Devi, she was the spiritual consort of Sri Ramakrishna Paramahamsa, and after his passing in 1886 became the spiritual head of the lineage and Order he brought together, which today has centers all over the world. Yet, it was not merely her status as his wife that made her thus, but increasing recognition by Sri Ramakrishna's disciples and others that she embodied the singular Reality known as the Divine Mother of the Universe. Though a simple village woman, nearly illiterate, a purdah widow observing caste rules, she nonetheless had the ability to penetrate to the heart of any issue, set aside socio-cultural strictures instantly as the circumstances required, and bestow spiritual insight with a look, a touch, a thought. She embodies the compassionate Motherhood of God.

Those who are acquainted or even well-acquainted with Holy Mother's life will revel in all the new details. It is an utter banquet that can satisfy our hunger and thirst for her divine presence and love. She simultaneously connects intimately to our daily lives through her ordinary activities and experiences, while engulfing us with the magnificence of her imminent divine reality. Did we long to hear more about her life with Sri Ramakrishna? It is given! Did we secretly wonder how she could be so attached to domestic family issues and still be looked upon as the final word in spirituality by Swamis Vivekananda, Brahmananda, and others? It is there in absolutely edifying examples. Perhaps we wanted to know about her samadhis, her wisdom words, or more about her relationships with Western women devotees – it is provided! And along with so much more, as well.

For Western women treading the path of spirituality, Holy Mother's life is a honeycomb of inspiration and loving wisdom. She immediately transcends the veil of culture and embraces us as her own; and in her vast spiritual affection, we understand the value of simplicity, what dedication, freedom, and spirituality really are, and how to be true every moment of our lives. Margaret Noble, known as Sister Nivedita, spent many intimate hours with Holy Mother and wrote on two different occasions: *"She really is, under the simplest, most unassuming guise, one of the strongest and greatest of women."* And also,*"...the stateliness of her courtesy and her great open mind are almost as wonderful as her sainthood. I have never known her to hesitate in giving utterance to large and generous judgement, however new or complex might be the question put before her."*

In the earlier works of Holy Mother's life, we have been introduced to her modesty and bashfulness and become acquainted with a selection of her simple and penetrating teachings. Written and/or edited as these are by the monks of the Ramakrishna Order, one cannot fail to notice and respond inwardly to the profound reverence for her as the *"Sangha Janani"* (Mother of the Sangha) and the *Shakti* (Power) of Sri Ramakrishna. But one also might have felt a certain reticence to exposing her fully to the public. She kept herself veiled, after all, even before her spiritual sons. Now, after nearly 100 years since Holy Mother left her physical form, it seems she has compassionately decided to put aside this veil so we may gaze with love and fascinated awe upon her entire life in intimate and astounding detail — and the result is this book. As Swami Chetanananda writes, "I deeply felt that this project would help me accomplish two goals: first, it would engage my mind in meditating on Holy Mother for a long period; second, her sublime life and practical teachings would inspire people in this joyless world."

"Let me tell you something. No one will understand me as long as I am alive. They will know only afterwards." - Sri Sarada Devi

Our gratitude will ever be to the author for bringing us into his liladhyan upon Sri Sarada Devi, the Holy Mother.

Annapurna Sarada

SRV Associations — Babaji's Teaching Schedule, 2016

SRV Hawai'i
Administrative Office
PO Box 1364
Honoka'a, HI 96727

SRV Associations'
website: www.srv.org
email: srvinfo@srv.org
Phone: 808-990-3354

SRV Oregon
1922 SE 42nd Ave.,
Portland, OR 97215
Ph: 503-774-2410

SRV San Francisco
465 Brussels Street
San Francisco, CA 94134
Ph: 415-468-4680

March, 2016

SRV San Francisco (Meditation, 6 to 7 am)
3/4 Fri 7:00pm Arati/Satsang with Babaji
3/5 Sat 9:30am Class: Svetasvatara Upanisad
        7:00pm **Sri Ramakrishna Birth Puja/Sivaratri**
3/6 Sun 9:30am Class: Svetasvatara Upanisad

SRV Oregon (Call for meditation times)
3/11 Fri 7:00 pm Satsang with Babaji
3/12 Sat 9:30am Class: Adhyatma Upanisad
         6:00pm **Sri Ramakrishna Birth Puja**
3/13 Sun 9:30am Class: Adhyatma Upanisad
3/16 Wed 7:00pm Principles of the Upanisads, with Anurag

3/17 - 3/21 — SRV Spring Equinox Retreat, Seattle

SRV Winter-Spring Retreat, 3/17 - 3/21, Seattle, WA
Subject: Sri Ramakrishna & Kundalini Shakti
(arrive Thursday night, 17th, depart Monday at noon)
For details, see Retreat Pages

May, 2016

SRV San Francisco (Meditation, 6 to 7 am)
5/13 Fri 7:00pm Arati/Satsang
5/14 Sat 9:30am Class: Svetasvatara Upanisad
         7:00pm SRV Puja
5/15 Sun 9:30am Class: Svetasvatara Upanisad

SRV Oregon (Call for meditation times)
5/20 Fri 6:00pm **Book Release: Cosmic Quintuplications**
                Book Signing Event with Babaji, Plus Music
                At Opening to Life, 407 NE 12th
5/21 Sat 9:30am Class: Key Teachings of Tibetan Buddhism
         6:00pm SRV Puja, Siva Puja
5/22 Sun 9:30am Class: Adhyatma Upanisad
5/25 Wed 7:00pm Principles of the Upanisads, with Anurag

5/26 - 5/30 — SRV Spring Retreat, Stevenson, WA

Memorial Day Weekend Retreat — 5/26 - 30
Stevenson, WA
Subject:
Vedanta & Neo-Vedanta
of Shankara & Vivekananda
Location: Windwood Waters (Wind River Region)
(arrive Thursday evening, 26th, depart Monday at noon)
For details, see Retreat Pages

July, 2016

SRV San Francisco (Meditation, 6 to 7 am)
7/15 Fri SRV SF Summer Retreat Begins at Foresthill, CA.

SRV American River Retreat over Gurupurnima
July 14th, eve - July 20th, noon – Foresthill, CA
Subject: Saints, Sages, Seers, Saviors & Their Teachings
Plus: Chanting, Memorization, & Discourse on the Sri Siva Sankirtanam
Plus: Western Women Pioneers of Vedanta with Annapurna Sarada
(arrive Thursday night, 14th, depart Wednesday at noon)
For details, see Retreat Pages

SRV Oregon (Call for meditation times)
7/23 Sat 9:30am Class: Adhyatma Upanisad
         6:00pm **Gurupurnima Puja**
7/24 Sun 9:30am Class: Adhyatma Upanisad
7/27 Wed 7:00pm Principles of the Upanisads, with Anurag
7/29 Fri 6:00 pm Satsang with Babaji
7/30 Sat 9:30 am Class: Adhyatma Upanisad
         6:00pm SRV Puja, Siva Puja
7/31 Sun 9:30 am Class: Adhyatma Upanisad
8/3 Wed 7:00pm Western Women Pioneers of Vedanta

8/5 - 8/7 – SRV Weekend Seminar with Satsang
Subject: The Guru/Shishya Relationship
Friday Satsang at 7 pm, & 2 classes Sat., 2 classes Sun.

September/October, 2016

SRV San Francisco (Meditation, 6 to 7 am)
9/30 Fri 7:00pm Arati/Satsang
10/1 Sat 9:30am Class: The Goddess Upanisads
         7:00pm **Durga Puja**
10/2 Sun 9:30am Class: Svetasvatara Upanisad

SRV Oregon (Call for meditation times)
10/7 Fri 7:00pm Satsang with Babaji
10/8 Sat 9:30am Class: Adhyatma Upanisad
         6:00pm **Durga Puja**
10/9 Sun 9:30am Class: Adhyatma Upanisad
10/12 Wed 7:00pm Principles of the Upanisads, with Anurag

SRV Fall Retreat — 10/13 - 10/17
Seattle, WA
SRV Kali Durga Lakshmi Retreat
Subject: The Seven Goddess Upanisads
(arrive Thursday evening, 13th, depart Monday at noon)
For details, see Retreat Pages

Visit srv.org for all retreat details
Weekend Classes webcasted, 9:30 am to 12:30 pm, Pacific Time

---

* Vedanta for Teens & Children
at SRV Oregon and SRV San Francisco
Contact Annapurna Sarada — Ph: 808-990-3354

SRV Associations — Babaji's Teaching Schedule, 2016
SRV Hawai'i Ashram, Big Island

Annual Hawaii Retreat
over Martin Luther King Weekend
Location: Puna, Big Island of Hawaii
Making Crucial Spiritual Connections II
January 15-18, 2016

Sunday Live Streaming Classes, 2:30 - 5:30pm
Hawaii SRV Ashram   Directions: Call: 808-990-3354

- **Key Teachings of the Bhagavad Gita**
  January 24, 31, & Feb 7, 14, 21, 2016
- **Key Teachings of Zen Buddhism**
  April 3, 10, 17, 24 & May 1st
- **Spiritual Transmission of Swami Vivekananda**
  June 12, 19, 26, & July 3rd
- **India's Sanatana Dharma**
  August 21, 28, & September 4, 11, 18th
- **Topic: Meeting Mother Kali**
  October 30, & November 6, 13, 20, 27th

Notice:
Our 2016 schedule is subject to change.
Please check the calendar on our website
www.srv.org
and sign our e-list at classes for notifications
or read our e-newsletter, Mundamala.
You can also contact your local SRV center:
Hawaii & Oregon: 808-990-3354
San Francisco: 415-468-4680

Check www.srv.org for Hawaii retreats
or see our Retreats Pages in the back of this issue

Sign up for:
- SRV Magazine: Nectar of Non-Dual Truth
- Raja Yoga email study with Babaji
- SRV's Facebook page
- SRV's YouTube channel: Teaching videos

* Please call or inquire about our Children's Classes
Contact Annapurna Sarada — Phone 808-990-3354

SRV Hawai'i Administrative Office:
PO Box 1364
Honoka'a, HI 96727
Ph: 808-990-3354

SRV Associations' website:
www.srv.org
email:
srvinfo@srv.org

See our SRV Facebook Page   facebook.com/srv.vedanta

SRV Associations Website
www.srv.org
srvinfo@srv.org

SRV On The Web
Visit www.srv.org to find:

SRV's Livestream Channel
Webcast Time Zone Schedule
SRV's YouTube Channel Class Series
- Advaita of the Avatars
- Devotion of Nonseparation
- The Wisdom Particle
- Non-Touch Yoga
- Shakta-Advaita-vada
- Satsangs with Babaj

Explore our Website links to find:
- Sanskrit Chants to learn/practice
- Devotional Songs
- Audio Discourses

Teachings:
- Articles
- Raja Yoga Sutras Study
- SRV's Teachings for Youth/Children
- Podcasts

Magazine:
- Order back issues of Nectar
- View our online archive of Nectar
- Order back issues of Nectar

News & Events
- Mundamala – SRV's e-newsletter
  Full of teachings and more

SRV Associations — Retreats for 2016

SRV Winter/Spring Equinox Retreat
March 17th - 21st, 2016, Seattle, Washington
Retreat Topic: Sri Ramakrishna & Kundalini Yoga

One of India's most popular and controversial of all yogic pathways, and probably its most mystical, Kundalini Yoga is both time-tested and verified by the luminaries as being a definitive method for the attainment of full Enlightenment. When expertly guided and properly applied, the awakening of mankind's innate spirituality is certain. Utilizing his new book entitled *Reclaiming Kundalini Yoga*, Babaji Bob Kindler will guide the retreatants on a hands-on inner journey designed to awaken the sleeping inner potential of the drowsy and unreceptive soul.

*"Know for certain that there can be no appreciable advancement
for the spiritual aspirant until Kundalini Shakti is awakened."
Sri Ramakrishna Paramahamsa*

*Awake, Mother, Awake! How long Thou hast been asleep in the Lotus of the Muladhara!
Fulfill Thy secret function Mother, rise to the thousand-petalled lotus within the head,
Where mighty Siva has His dwelling; swiftly pierce the six lotuses
And take away my grief, O Essence of Consciousness! – Gospel of Sri Ramakrishna*

Texts: *Reclaiming Kundalini Yoga & Gospel of Sri Ramakrishna*   **Location:** Seattle, Washington
Arrival: Thursday, March 17, after dinner and by 9:00pm   **Departure:** Monday, March 21st, at 12:00pm
Tuition (all inclusive): $350; students $175   **Registration:** Starts now. Tuition is due by March 1st
Financial hardship? Call 808-990-3354   **Register by email:** srvinfo@srv.org or by phone 808-990-3354

SRV Spring Retreat Over Memorial Day
May 26 – 30th, 2016, Wind River region, Washington
Subject: Vedanta & Neo-Vedanta of Shankara and Vivekananda

The face of Vedanta in 700 A.D. when Shankara resurrected and reestablished it in India after the decline of Buddhism has changed with the arrival of Swami Vivekananda on the contemporary scene. The great swami has now made its intrinsically universal message broadcast in all countries, and rendered its timeless tenets accessible to all beings at all stations of life.

In SRV's Spring retreat at Windwood Waters near the Columbia River Gorge in Washington state, the underground river of Vedanta will surface once again, bringing its healing Waters of Life upwards in a fountain of Truth to nourish all thirsty souls — just as it did in Shankara's time in India in 700 A.D.

Location: Windwood Waters retreat site near Stevenson, WA
Arrival: Thursday, May 26, between 4:00 & 9:00 pm
Departure: Monday, May 30, 1:00pm
Registration: Starts now. Tuition and lodging fees are due by May 7th
Register by email: srvinfo@srv.org or by phone 808-990-3354
Costs: Tuition and meals: $390; Students:: $200 (lodging additional)
Lodging: private room single, $240; private room shared with 1 - 2 others, $160/person;
semi-private lodge sleeping, $120*; Tenting, $80*   *bring your own bedding/towels

SRV American River Retreat, 2016
July 14 – 20, 2016, Forest Hill, CA

- **Saints, Sages, Seers, Saviors & Their Teachings, & Sri Sivanam Sankirtanam Chanting**
  Plus: Western Women Pioneers of Vedanta, with Annapurna Sarada
- Live in holy company for a full week – meditating, studying, serving, and growing together.
- Each morning begins with chanting from the Bhagavad Gita prior to meditation.
- Daily classes include essential teachings of Yoga, Vedanta, Tantra, and Sankhya.
- Afternoons include explorations and swimming/sunning along the American River.
- Afternoon Chela Dharma class for teens and young adults.
- Evening devotions at the altar, singing and chanting, meditation, and satsang.
- <u>Concurrent Children's Retreat</u> — Children, ages 6 to approximately 13 have their own simultaneous retreat. Activities include "salute to the sun," morning ritual, meditation, Vedic stories and lessons, and arts and crafts.

Location: Private land in Foresthill, California near the American River
Arrival: Arrive by 6pm, Thursday evening, July 14th
Last day of retreat: Wednesday, July 20 (approximately noon, clean up follows)
Tuition: all inclusive
  Adults: $636 (full retreat) $275 (weekend, arrive Friday) $110/day
  Children/Students: $300 (full retreat) $140 (weekend, arrive Friday) $55/day
Registration: starts now and tuition is due by Sunday, <u>July 3rd</u>
Financial hardship? Call 808-990-3354 to discuss options
Register by email: srvinfo@srv.org or by phone 808-990-3354

Autumn Retreat Over Lakshmi Puja
October 13 – 17th, 2016, Location: Seattle, Washington
Subject: The Seven Goddess Upanisads

Similar to SRV's Fall retreat of 2015, wherein the Devi Upanisad was presented and studied in depth, Babaji Bob Kindler will take another of the Seven Goddess Upanisads up for examination and contemplation.

Location: Seattle, Washington
Arrival: Thursday, October 13 after dinner, at 9:00pm
Departure: Monday, October 18, 12:00pm
Tuition (all-inclusive): Adults: $350: Students: $175
Lodging: Private room single, $240; Private room shared, $160/person
Registration: Tuition and other fees are due by <u>October 1st</u>

Plus: SRV Seminar in 2016
The Guru-Shishya Relationship According to Lord Vasishtha

"They attain to the Supreme Self who study the Atmajnan scriptures with an able preceptor from their early youth." Lord Vasishtha

Location: SRV Oregon Ashram in Portland
Friday, August 5: 7:00 PM – Satsang
Saturday, August 6: 6:00am – 5:00pm (breakfast/dinner)
Sunday, August 7: 6:00am – 5:00pm (breakfast only)
Tuition: $220; student, $110

Accommodations: <u>This is a non-residential seminar</u>
Contact us if you would like assistance with lodging. 808-990-3354 // srvinfo@srv.org

The "In The Spirit" Interviews of Lex Hixon

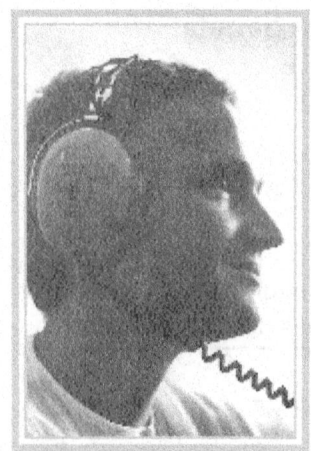

Lex Hixon

From the early 1970's on through the late 1980's, Lex Hixon hosted a radio program in New York City that was unprecedented in its depth, scope, insight and unique creativity. First entitled "In The Spirit," it also later appeared under the titles of "Body/Mind/Spirit," and "Spirit/Mind/Body."

On this long running inspirational program that spanned over two decades and which was duly sponsored in listener-supported fashion on WBAI Radio, Lex interviewed educators, healers, clergy, authors, artists, psychics, spiritual leaders and others.

As a list, the fruit of this selfless work reads like a comprehensive Who's Who of the spiritual, artistic and intellectual heart and mind of both Eastern and Western cultures. With subtle tenderness and insight, though never lacking the penetrating edge which makes for excellent broadcasting, Lex welcomed the orthodox and the unorthodox, the conservative and the radical, the famous and the obscure, the popular and the controversial, the powerful and the humble, the aggressive and the retiring.

Included in this copious series are interviews with gurus, yogis, swamis, priests, roshis, rabbis/rebbes, sheikhs, lamas, rinpoches, poets, musicians, psychics, occultists, authors, writers, teachers, politicians, businessmen and more.

- Over 325 Titles to choose from
- Individual CD's are available
- Trio sets
- Full set prices
- List of all titles available upon request
- Highest quality materials used

"IN THE SPIRIT" CD Trio Sets
Choice selections from the cassette series on CD

Buddhist
B1 - Tibetan
Dalai Lama
Kalu Rinpoche
Trungpa Rinpoche

B2 - Zen
Eido Roshi
Soen Roshi
Maesumi Roshi

B3 - American
Phillip Kapleau
Bernie Glassman
Robert Thurman

Christianity
C1 - Mother Teresa
Padre Pio
Meister Ekhart

Islam/Sufism
IS1 - Sheikh Muzaffer
Guru Bawa
Sheikh Nur Al Jerrahi

Judaism
J1 - Rabbi Shlomo Carlebach
Rebbe Gedalia
Rabbi Zalman Schachter

J2 - Rebbi Meyer Fund
Rabbi Dovid Din
Rabbi Lynn Gotleib

Lex Hixon
H1 - On the Haj
On the Karmapa
On Himself

Professors & Authors
PA1 - Huston Smith
Christopher Isherwood
Jack Cornfield

PA2 - David Spangler
Alan Watts
Alan Ginsberg

Shamanism/Amer. Indian
SI1 - Oh Shinnah
Dhani Thorna
Don Juan

Vedic
V1 - Sri Ramakrishna

V2 - Ramakrishna Order Swamis
Vivekananda
Nikhilananda
Prabhavananda

V3 - Swamis
Dayananda
Muktananda
Satchitananda

V4 - Special Luminaries
Ramana Maharshi
Sri Aurobindo
Krishnamurti

V5 - Spiritual Teachers
Meher Baba
Sri Chinmoy
Ram Das

V6 - Divine Mother of the Universe

Postal Orders: Jai Ma Music, PO Box 380, Paauilo, HI 96776
Email Orders: srvinfo@srv.org
Phone Orders: 808-990-3354
Website: www.srv.org

Advaita satya amritam

NECTAR
of Non-Dual Truth

Donation/Order Form
Suggested donation $15 per issue

Nectar #31 is available for free if you write, email, or call for a copy before Feb. 1st, 2016
Your generous donations make Nectar available to others and help us to widen our distribution.

Those who donate $15 or more for the next issue will be added to our subscriber's list
- ❏ Please send me/my friend a free copy of the next issue of Nectar.
- ❏ Send me ___ copies to give to friends or a spiritual center of my choice.
- ❏ I am enclosing the names of persons/centers I want to receive Nectar. Fill out the back of this form.

- ❏ *I want to help keep Nectar in print. ($200 and up)*

Please fill out the back side of this form and mail it with your check to:
SRV Associations, PO Box 1364, Honokaa, HI 96727
MasterCard or Visa accepted ◆ Make checks payable to: SRV Associations
808-990-3354 ◆ srvinfo@srv.org ◆ www.srv.org

#31

Advaita satya amritam

NECTAR
of Non-Dual Truth

Donation/Order Form
Suggested donation $15 per issue

Nectar #31 is available for free if you write, email, or call for a copy before Feb. 1st, 2016
Your generous donations make Nectar available to others and help us to widen our distribution.

Those who donate $15 or more for the next issue will be added to our subscriber's list
- ❏ Please send me/my friend a free copy of the next issue of Nectar.
- ❏ Send me ___ copies to give to friends or a spiritual center of my choice.
- ❏ I am enclosing the names of persons/centers I want to receive Nectar. Fill out the back of this form.

- ❏ *I want to help keep Nectar in print. ($200 and up)*

Please fill out the back side of this form and mail it with your check to:
SRV Associations, PO Box 1364, Honokaa, HI 96727
MasterCard or Visa accepted ◆ Make checks payable to: SRV Associations
808-990-3354 ◆ srvinfo@srv.org ◆ www.srv.org

#31

Advaita satya amritam

NECTAR
of Non-Dual Truth

Donation/Order Form
Suggested donation $15 per issue

Nectar #31 is available for free if you write, email, or call for a copy before Feb. 1st, 2016
Your generous donations make Nectar available to others and help us to widen our distribution.

Those who donate $15 or more for the next issue will be added to our subscriber's list
- ❏ Please send me/my friend a free copy of the next issue of Nectar.
- ❏ Send me ___ copies to give to friends or a spiritual center of my choice.
- ❏ I am enclosing the names of persons/centers I want to receive Nectar. Fill out the back of this form.

- ❏ *I want to help keep Nectar in print. ($200 and up)*

Please fill out the back side of this form and mail it with your check to:
SRV Associations, PO Box 1364, Honokaa, HI 96727
MasterCard or Visa accepted ◆ Make checks payable to: SRV Associations
808-990-3354 ◆ srvinfo@srv.org ◆ www.srv.org

#31

Your Information:

Name: _____

Address: _____

City, State, Zip: _____

Email: _____

Additional Address: (please use a sheet of paper for more addresses)

Name: _____

Address: _____

City, State, Zip: _____

Email: _____

Do you wish to pay by Mastercard or Visa?

Card No.: _____ **Amount:** _____

Exp. date: _____ **Phone no.:** _____

Signature: _____

Questions? call SRV Associations: 808-990-3354

Your Information:

Name: _____

Address: _____

City, State, Zip: _____

Email: _____

Additional Address: (please use a sheet of paper for more addresses)

Name: _____

Address: _____

City, State, Zip: _____

Email: _____

Do you wish to pay by Mastercard or Visa?

Card No.: _____ **Amount:** _____

Exp. date: _____ **Phone no.:** _____

Signature: _____

Questions? call SRV Associations: 808-990-3354

Your Information:

Name: _____

Address: _____

City, State, Zip: _____

Email: _____

Additional Address: (please use a sheet of paper for more addresses)

Name: _____

Address: _____

City, State, Zip: _____

Email: _____

Do you wish to pay by Mastercard or Visa?

Card No.: _____ **Amount:** _____

Exp. date: _____ **Phone no.:** _____

Signature: _____

Questions? call SRV Associations: 808-990-3354